THE PETIT AI

THE PETIT ALBERT

The Marvellous Secrets of The Little Albert: English Edition

ORIGINAL EDITION CIRCA 18th CENTURY
NEW ENGLISH EDITION 2016
EDITED AND ILLUSTRATED BY TARL WARWICK

THE PETIT ALBERT

DISCLAIMER AND COPYRIGHT

This text is to in no way be construed as able to diagnose, treat, or cure any disease. Some of the rituals within this work are hazardous and should not be conducted.

The original French edition of the Petit Albert is in the public domain.

All rights reserved for this English edition, its illustrations, and its cover art.

THE PETIT ALBERT

INTRODUCTION AND FOREWORD

The vast importance of the *Petit Albert* and its natural, partially separate counterpart the *Grand Albert* within the French cycle of occult literature cannot possibly be overstated. Multiple editions of this same work have been released, but with the exception of limited or hardcover editions, nowhere before have I seen it translated properly into easily understood English. As such, this edition was necessary, in order to open up the work to a new audience.

The material of the French Cycle of grimoires roughly falls into three major categories, or so it seems from my own (extensive) research into grimoires, especially those of the Renaissance and Enlightenment. There are those works which dwell upon the talismanic arts- the creation of external objects of an enchanted nature, then there are those which better fit with the Solomonic works dating well into the past with the original creation of the famed *Testament of Solomon*- that this second category borrows heavily from the same and from other former works is clear. The final category is comprised of those works dwelling mostly on folk ritualism and folk magick- not always just from France itself, often from lands it was actively encountering during the dawn of colonialism, and often from other European lands.

The Petit Albert is a fusion of all three of these categories and as such is composed of a rather broad

THE PETIT ALBERT

collection involving many folk rituals, potions, simple incantations, talismanic creation, observations of the celestial, and many other workings. Like the *Grimorium Verum* it has a diabolical twist to it that is not found in many grimoires; the laypeople of the modern age often conflate the term with meaning, specifically, "leather bound, demonic book specifically for black magick workings, employed by ugly old hags or black robed devil worshipers."

In many such works the concept of obtaining wealth and love is predominant; here there is no exception, at least in the first few sections of the work, which deal specifically with those subjects- it then delves into talismans, with a lengthy segment on the same which approaches the level of detail given by the *Black Pullet* if it is stripped of its "Mysterious Turkish mage" back story until only the recipes for the talismans remain.

As you can probably tell from the last few paragraphs the work relates heavily to all of these other titles; the Petit Albert is indeed a hodge-podge of different systems. This is not to denigrate it- quite the opposite- it produces a cross section of the eras' folkish ways and gives insight into more than just one interpretation of one system as many works do. In this way, it is perhaps the most valuable grimoire ever produced, and is at least as infamous for its content as the *Red Dragon* which is smaller but shares in its capability to discuss destructive occultism without hesitation.

Moreover, we have here one of only two works

THE PETIT ALBERT

which I am aware of in which the author themselves claims to have personally witnessed such works firsthand- in one such case, here, it is a warning against charlatans using mandrake roots to fool people into paying them for fortune telling, but elsewhere several real-world landmarks are mentioned as having been protected or influenced in some way by the talismans spoken of here.

The work also shows the increasing familiarity of cosmopolitan, rising France with its Northern neighbors, with its (lengthy) expose on the topic of gnomes, elves, salamanders, and other such creatures- here, though, instead of an anthropological study of sorts, the material relates almost entirely to mining and to obtaining rich ore seams or buried treasure, and to avoiding harm which might come from disturbing or infuriating various quasi-cosmic, quasi-cryptozoological creatures possessed of volition.

Part of this work is blatantly scientific as opposed to, as we would say today, "occult" or "mystic" in nature as well. In these past eras, simplistic scientific workings were indeed considered to be a form of (sometimes acceptable) witchery. Much as grimoires were begrudgingly tolerated by the church, these rites were tolerated by everyone despite their variously mystic, angellic, or demonic overtones. Here, thus, are recipes for fattening livestock, protecting crops, protecting against torture or fire, healing various sicknesses (a medicinal list of herbs and minerals which I judge to be at least potentially of some effect- I've studied herbalism for years), and many other workings which must have seemed miraculous.

THE PETIT ALBERT

The Petit Albert also covers alchemy of a sort- the making of counterfeit currency, the making of fake gold, the increasing of gold and silver by heating, mixing, and amalgamating with other materials. Unlike some works this book is honest about the process if you read between the lines; it is not claiming that gold is made, merely that something physically similar is made, and that it will fool merchants and nobles alike if the alchemist has the skill. Not content to supply the reader with fake gold or copper, the author helpfully instructed them as well how to take valuable materials such as musk and ambergris (the real kind, not modern, synthetic, cheap substitutes, hence the cost then and now) and increase them- by mixing and brewing the same with various other materials, creating an artificial component of the same which nobody would be able to differentiate from the real stuff.

The most strange part of the entire work though is perhaps the construction of a pair of two-way compasses meant to communicate oveer long distances. Here, two compass needles are carved from one strongly magnetic rock and placed on identical boxes with letters and numbers engraved upon them, such that, according to the author, if one needle is moved, the other will do the same. The basic concept is interesting because it roughly mimicks what would come a century later when actual long distance communication was developed; the concept of standardized characters for the same, that is. Whether or not people constructing such boxes were fooling themselves or interacting with some form of magnetic disturbance is not known.

THE PETIT ALBERT

Lastly it behooves us to consider the hand of glory which is spoken of here with greater length than any other work to my knowledge which bothers to mention it at all. This pickled "hand of a thief who was hung" seems to have been the pride and joy of Continental occultists from that era just as pants made entirely out of a skinned mans' legs and hips were all the rage to Scandinavian shaman some centuries before. This motif, of the hand of glory, is diabolical enough to have been mentioned in fictional literature and film alike; for a slightly fictional-contemporary and somewhat occult-inspired look at such ritualism I recommend the film *Brotherhood of the Wolf* which was and is excellent for entertainment value as well; such items and references are made there.

It is not explicitly known how the hand of glory was meant to be crafted; various accounts exist, and while the fact that the hand had to be from a thief and preserved is common across all accounts, the method of preservation and the location of the thief's death are different. This work almost surely incorporates a folkish twist to the same, substituting perhaps any expensive or uncommon preserving ingredients in whatever primordial source influenced such rites to begin with, with cheaper, more easily obtained ones.

Of all grimoires this might be the foremost. Regardless, its content is indeed worthy of inclusion on any must-read list of occult literature.

THE PETIT ALBERT

TABLE OF CONTENTS

A Warning to the Reader
The Treasure of Wondrous Secrets
To Obtain Love
Defending Against the Curse of the Lanyard
To Tie the Lanyard
To Moderate the Female Sex Drive
To Determine and Protect Chastity
To Know if a Girl is Pure or Corrupted
To Restore Virginity
To Prevent your Woman from Fornicating
To Rejuvinate Wrinkled Skin Due to Childbirth
For Women to Dream of Seeing the Man They Should Marry
For Men to Do the Same
To Keep Your Man Loyal
To Cause a Girl to Dance Naked
To Prosper at Gambling
To Prosper at Fishing
To Keep Birds Out of Your Crops
To Hunt Birds Effectively
To Prosper at Caring for Birds
To Prevent Dogs from Becoming Aggressive
Another Method, to Prevent Rabies
To Ward Off Wolves
To Prevent Drunkenness
To Restore Stale Wine
To Make Excellent Vinegar
To Make Good Liquers
An Excellent and Fast Hippocras
The True Water of Armenia
Growing Sweet Melons
Growing Good Grapes

THE PETIT ALBERT

To Prosper at Growing Wheat
To Prevent Animals from Destroying Your Crops
To Divine Whether Next Years Planting Will be Good
To Defend Against Illness
Ancient Talismans and the Usage Thereof
Talisman of the Sun for Sunday
Talisman of the Moon for Monday
Talisman of Mars for Tuesday
Talisman of Mercury for Wednesday
Talisman of Jupiter for Thursday
Talisman of Venus for Friday
Talisman of Saturn for Saturday
Forming Plaques For the Talismans, In Mercury
Formulating Talismans Used by Other Kabbalists
Salamanders, Gnomes, Nymphs, and Sylphs
Oration Of the Salamanders
Perfume For Sunday And the Sun
Perfume For Monday And the Moon
Perfume For Tuesday And Mars
Perfume For Wednesday And Mercury
Perfume For Friday And Venus
Perfume For Saturday And Saturn
Fake Mandrakes
Natural Processes Of Interest
The Hand of Glory
To Make a Person Insensible to Torture
An Ointment Which Protects Against Fire
Making Ardent Water
Making Greek Fire
To Create Peace
The Secret Garter For Travelers
The Secret Stick For Travelers
The Secret to Making Horses Travel Quickly
To Make an Angry Horse Tame
To Cause the Horse to Appear Deceased

THE PETIT ALBERT

The Ring of Invisibility
To See Fascinating Things With the Ring
To Manufacture Other Rings Under the Auspices of the Planets
The Hours of the Day and Night
The Philosophers Regarding Talismans
Balm Oil Extracted From Heavenly Water
Balm to Prevent Plague
To Remove Rotten Teeth Painlessly
To Cure Gunshots or Other Wounds
To Treat Sprains of the Feet
Of Mandrakes
Explanations of the Heavenly Talismans
A Healing Powder
Making Gold Artificially
To Precipitate Gold
To Dissolve Gold
Turning Lead Into Gold
To Create Fake Money Using Tin
Using Borax To Melt Gold
Creating Imitation Pearls
To Create Fake Musk That Will Be Seen As Real Musk
Making Fake Ambergris
Making Excellent Incense Pellets
Softening Ivory
Obtaining Grass Twine
Breaking Iron Easily
A Ring That Heals Palsy
Talismans To Protect Against Dangerous Animals
Explanation and Engravings of the Talismans
Argent Vive Of Hungary
Making A Wash To Cure Facial Blemishes
A Powder To Exfoliate The Face
A Soap For Faces and Hands Alike
Making Holy Water
The Light of the Hand of Glory

THE PETIT ALBERT

A Secret Compass For Long Distance Communication
To Fire a Rifle With Great Accuracy and Power
A Serum To Preserve Life
Planting Tree Branches To Make Them Grow
Making Much Soap
Increasing Saffron
Increasing Black Pepper
Increasing Wax
Increasing Musk
Dying Hair
Making A Fine Gold Varnish
Healing A Husky Throat
Cleaning the Teeth and Gums
Preventing Foul Breath
Curing A Bad Fever
A Secret To Maintain Good Health
To Determine Whether A Patient Shall Live or Die
Curing Dropsy
Curing Fistulas
Curing Pox Scars
Curing Bladder Stones
Curing Colic
Curing Urination Problems
Curing Oedemas
Curing Stomach Pains

THE PETIT ALBERT

A Warning to the Reader

Here is a new edition of the Wonderful Natural Secrets of the Little Albert, known in Latin by the title Libellus Alberti Parvi Lucii of mirabilibus Arcanis naturae: the author was one of those noble and wise men accused of witchery by the ignorant masses; (it was formerly the fate of all the great minds who possessed something extraordinary in science, as they were treated like magicians.) Perhaps that is why this little treasure has become so rare; because the superstitious reject its use, it's almost lost completely, for some wealthy people in the world have been curious enough (those which desire to obtain it) to offer more than a thousand guilders one copy yet failed to obtain one. We have discovered this work only recently in the library of a very great man who was pleased to give, not to deprive the public of such a rich treasure. It can now be obtained for a smaller sum and used for great profit. The curious will not mind the old and rudimentary language of this book; we preferred to leave it as we found it, rather than to change something, for fear of altering its true meaning. Besides, we will not be sorry that we have added to the end of this treasure, additional wondrous secrets, given by a person of great experience. And as it is often talked about in this book, some secret hours of the planets will be found at the end of this work in tables that mark the time of sunrise for every day of the year, in order not to deceive the hours that each planet governs, for one must know that time thereby is marked from dawn rather than the middle of the night as some believe erroneously.

THE PETIT ALBERT

The Treasure Of Wondrous Secrets

Those with curiosity, who wish to enjoy the most rare and most hidden secrets of nature, must, with openness of heart, listen carefully to what is written here in these pages.

It may well be called a universal secret, because it contains in its pages many wonders able to please all mankind. The noble as the commoner; merchant as the footsoldier; the warrior as peaceful; the squire as damsel; corrupted woman as a virgin, and above all the good conductor of his family, will take all that into my own experiences have proven to their advantage, and to satisfy their inclinations and enable their greatest desires.

However, in order to keep some methodical order in this book, and to make it more pleasant and helpful to my readers, I will distinguish each of the materials separately, lest the indiscreet mixture brings an embarrassing confusion. I mean, when I discuss, for example, the secrets of love or war, I will proceed with the content immediately, and without interruption, when I am giving these topics, or anything on the topic of natural science. I list elsewhere a few secrets that are right to love or war, I warn my readers, indicating the places where they can find these secrets.

It is good to similarly warn my readers that, while these may seem supreme secrets which I offer them in this small volume, they will not supercede the occult forces of nature; that is to say, of all created beings that are scattered in this vast universe, whether in heaven, in the air, on land or in the water. For so it is written that the sage will rule the stars, by his prudence, and it shall be seen that the stars by their gentle influences will benefit the wise and instruct through their ascendancy.

Now it is necessary to know the arrangements and rising of the stars in their course; for other forces are subjugated to these. As well as the stars it is commonly understood that the planets have their own day in the course of the week; the Sun for Sunday, Moon for Monday, Mars for Tuesday, Mercury for Wednesday, Jupiter for Thursday, Venus for Friday, Saturn for Saturday.

Those who have not studied in the sublime philosophy of science and astronomy must do so, or else consult astrologers or use a good almanac when they want to practice some secrets here which are dependent upon or in conjunction to the stars, so that the accuracy that they will bring in the operation they will do, will create a proper outcome.

These are not attributed to magic or devilry, though in some of the wonderful secrets that I will give are used certain words or figures; because they have their virtue and efficiency regardless of magic, and ancient Hebrew sages have used it within their own religion. The chroniclers of France tell us that Charlemagne received from Pope a little book which was composed only of figures and mysterious words, which this prince happily utilized upon many occasions; this small book is titled, enchiridium Leonis papae. The wonders that this short work has produced in support of those who have used it, have made it notorious despite those who wanted to disparage the book as superstitious.

Finally I warn my readers that they will find nothing common or trivial in this this little book; it is like an extract and elixir that aids in the improving of nature, as well as far more wonderful in its occult virtues. I have let myself be seduced to vanity at times by believing that I have performed these works under my own power. I confess that I have learned from the writings of famous philosophers that have most penetrated these arts with great power, applying everything secret within all of nature. I do not say this for the sake of my ego, for many others have done similarly.

To Obtain Love

Since there is nothing more natural for man to love and to be loved, I shall begin the content of my little treasure with secrets that lead to this end. It is no small task to invoke Venus and Cupid, which are the two dominant deities on this noble human passion. I will say that Mother Nature, who made all things for man, produced large numbers of creatures with days favorable to them in the success of their passion. It is often found at the front of the foal a piece of flesh, which I give here the figure, which is powerful for obtaining love because if we can have that piece of flesh the ancients called Hippomanes, we will make it dry in a clay pot finely glazed in a furnace. When dinner is being eaten, wear the piece of flesh on your body, and then doing touch the person you want to be loved by. Love can also be obtained by anyone, if they swallow only a piece of this flesh the size of two peas in a liqueur, jam or stew; the effect is certain. And as Friday is the day dedicated to Venus, which governs the mysteries of love, it will be good to perform such works on that day. Jean-Baptiste Porta has remarked upon the surprising properties of Hippomanes to cause love.

Another Method

On a Friday in spring, put to dry in the oven in a small pot, as stated above, the Hippomanes, along with the ears of a hare and the liver of a dove: Dry it into a powder and say the name of the person you wish to be loved by while it is drying. Consume a bit of the powder about the size of half a drachma, and if the effect does not follow the first time, repeat up to three times, and you will be loved.

Another Method

Live chastely for at least five or six days, and on the seventh, which will be on Friday, if possible; eat and drink hot foods which excite your passion. When you feel properly impassioned, draw close to have a conversation with the object of your passion, and you can do it properly. Stare at one another for the period of one Ave. Maria: because the visual rays are meeting each other, and are such powerful vehicles of love, they penetrate to the heart, and the greatest pride and the greatest insensitivity can not resist them. It is quite difficult to seduce a girl, who has a lover already, staring at a young man in a short space of time; but this may be done merely by saying jokingly, I learned a secret to guess by the eyes, if one is soon to be married, if you will live a long time, if you will be happy in his marriage, or some similar thing that flatters human curiosity, and which makes the mind and eyes to stare.

Another Method

Have a gold ring adorned with a small diamond, which has not been worn since it was first mined from the Earth, wrap a small piece of cloth and silk on it, and wear it for nine days and nine nights, with it between your shirt and chest. The ninth day, before sunrise, you will engrave, with a new chisel, the word "Sheva" upon the ring. Then obtain by any means three hairs from the person you want to be loved by, and you hold on to them, saying; Oh body, may you love me, and may your plans succeed as ardently as mine, by the power of Sheva! Then, you will tie these hairs together around the ring, ensuring the ring is almost completely entwined, and having wrapped the ring in silk fabric, you will wear again the wrapped ring for another six days in the same manner, and on the seventh day you will undo the hairs twined about it, and will then quickly receive the one you love: all parts of this operation must be done before the sunrise and while fasting.

Another Method

To say nothing that offends propriety, I will copy here what I have read, written by a very skilful physician, causing the human to passionately desire love through the use of an herb, especially as such an experience no one can cause without doing violence to nature that provides us enough other means. So we should rather use the herb which is called Enula campana.

While fasting, pluck one flower on the feast St. John in June, before sunrise, to dry, and then powder it with ambergris. Wear this upon your heart for nine days, and subsequently attempt to kiss the person you wish to be loved by, and the effect will follow. The dried heart of a dove or sparrow mixed with your blood and the blood of the person who you wish to be loved by, has the same effect.

Another Method

One can also have great success at procuring passion by the aid of talismans made under the constellation of Venus; I will give later in this little book of models etched therein, of seven talismans that can be done under the auspices of the seven planets, and I will discuss the methodical way of doing so, and the virtues they contain. We can see for the subject that I treat that of Venus. These talismans were composed by the wisest among Kabbalists, and are trained on the mysterious numbers, and suitable heiroglyphic figures with planets from which they derive their properties; they have been referred to as the stamps or seals of the planets or celestial powers.

Another Method

There are secrets of the so-called sages among Kabbalists, for gaining romantic love, and they are practiced in this way. You will go on a Friday morning before the sunrise into a fruit orchard, and pluck a fruit from the most beautiful apple tree which you can find; then you write with your blood on a small white piece of paper your first and last names, and upon the next line, the name and surname of the person you want to be loved by, and then you must take three of their hairs and will join them with three of yours that you used to link the little note you have written, one with another, on which there will be the word of Sheva, also written in your blood. Then, you must cut the apple in half; and you should put the halves along with your hair linked notes, and with two small sharp myrtle twigs, you will join properly the two apple halves around your note, and dry the apple in the oven, such that it becomes hard and dried such as dried apples are on Lent; Then you and wrap this in leaves of laurel and myrtle, and place it under the pillow where the loved one lays at night, without her knowledge, and in a short time you will obtain their love.

Another, To Secure Perpetual Love

It is not enough for a man to be loved by the woman only on one occasion, or temporarily; this passion ought to persist, and true love is indissoluble, and thus he needs to have a secret art to engage the woman which won't alter or diminish over time. Take the sinews of the foot of a wolf, and make a mixed ointment using also powdered amber and powdered reindeer moss; you will carry the ointment with you and you will sniff it from time to time in the presence of the woman you desire; she will love you increasingly.

Another Method

THE PETIT ALBERT

In some cases a woman will love her man if he is merely good at making love, he should therefore take precautions to safeguard his skills not only by good nourishment, but also by various ancient and modern secrets. Compose a balm composed of the ash of day lily, St. John's wort, and civet oil, and anoint the big toe of the left foot and the lower back one hour before attempting to court the lady and you will meet with success.

Another Method

This ointment consists of the fat of a young goat with ambergris and civet oil- which causes the same effect- and must be placed on the man's phallus before fornication because it produces a tickling which gives a wonderful pleasure to the woman in the action of coitus.

Another Method

If the husband finds his wife to be lacking passion in bed, and wishes to please her, because his own physical skills are lacking, then he should eat the kidneys of a crow, and a hare's belly, seasoned with fine spices, once in a while, with arugula, celery and rosehips with vinegar.

Defending Against The Curse of the Lanyard

Our elders assure us that these are effective defenses against the sorcery of the knotted lanyard; if fasting eat a roast with blessed salt, if you breathe the smoke of burning tooth of a man dead it has the same effect. The same effect also happens if put quicksilver in a torch of oat straw or wheat straw, this is placed under the pillow of the bed where the hexed individual sleeps. If a man and woman are afflicted with this charm, it is necessary to be healed; thus the man pees through his wifes wedding ring while she holds his.

To Tie the Lanyard

Have the penis of a newly killed wolf, and being close to the door of the one you want to bind, you will call them by their proper name, and as soon as he has answered, you will wrap the penis with a thread made from the white hairs of this same wolf, and it will hex the neighbors sexual abilities, just as the wolf's penis has now been rendered impotent. There are many ways to defend against, and even prevent, this kind of enchantment, you just have to wear a ring in which the right eye of a weasel is preserved as the centerpiece.

To Moderate the Female Sex Drive

Reduce a red bull's dried penis to powder, and add a bit of this powder, weighing about a half ounce, to a broth made of veal, lettuce, and purslane, and feed it to the immodest woman. This will modulate her sexual desires.

To Determine and Protect Chastity

Although the broth seasoned with lettuce and purslane are useful to dampen the ardor of lust, however, as they do not do so in all seasons, and this one meal may become boring, like the Israelites who bored with manna in the desert, nature has provided manifold other remedies. So you take powdered agate stone, and put this upon a belt that can be dipped in wolf fat, and we gird up the loins of this band as a belt. It can also be wrapped in a wolf skin for added effect; regardless, for a man, he should add to this the heart of a male quail, and for a woman, of a female quail.

To Know If A Girl Is Pure or Corrupted

You will reduce black coal to fine powder; you will take the weight of a shield in powdered coal to the girl. If the girl has been corrupted, it will be impossible for her to hold her urine, and she will need to urinate. If instead the girl is chaste, she will retain her urine. Amber, yellow or white, which is made into necklaces and rosaries, produces the same event, if it is used with the same preparation as the charcoal, or else porcelain seed, leaf cocklebur root, powdered, and the same in a broth to drink with liquor or other materials, they all serve the same.

Another Method

Have a white twine spun, and measure with this yarn size of the neck of the girl, and then you will double this measure, and you will hold both ends to the girl with your teeth, and you will extend the measure to pass her head through. If the head passes too easily, she is corrupt, if not, her purity is assured.

To Restore Virginity

Take a half ounce of turpentine, a little juice from macerated asparagus, mineral oil infused into a quarter ounce of lemon juice or juice of green plums, and fresh egg white with a little oatmeal: Make this all into a bolus that has some consistency, and you will put it in the vagina of the girl after defloration with goat milk and anointed ointment of white Rasis. You will not have practiced this secret four or five times, the girl will return to the state of virginity to deceive the matron who would wish to visit. Distilled water with lemon juice, being applied several days in the vagina of the girl, has the same effect if the ointment is applied as before.

To Prevent Your Woman From Fornicating

Those who are forced to be absent for a long time of their house, and which have women who have suspicious and subject practices, do the following for your safety. Take a little hair of the women, and powder it, and add it to honey, which you should apply to the woman's vagina. She will then have a very great distaste for sexual intercourse. If the husband wishes to experience the same temporary distaste he should powder his own hair, add it to the honey, and again have intercourse and will equally shun extramarital pleasures.

To Rejuvinate Wrinkled Skin Due to Childbirth

You shall compose an ointment with turpentine, milk, asparagus leaves, soft white cheese, and the powdered quartz, and having rubbed the stomach with a sponge soaked with lemon, apply a patch of that ointment on the stomach, and repeat this several times, and the marks of childbirth will wane.

For Women to Dream of Seeing the Man They Should Marry

You must have a small branch of the tree called poplar, and should bind this to a white piece of cord down with your pants. After putting under the bed where you have to sleep at night, rub your temples with a bit of blood from the hoopoe bird, and while lying say the following invocation.

The Prayer

Clementissime Kyrios, quod Abraham servo tuo dedisti uxorem Saram et filio ejus obedientissimo, admirabile per signum indicati Rebeccam uxorem: indica mihi ancillae tuae quem sim nuptura, virum, per Ministerium tuorum spirituum Balideth, Assaibi, Abumalith. Amen.

The next morning when you awake, get back in mind what you have seen in a dream during the night, and sleeping in if you did not see any man's appearance. You must continue during the night three Fridays in a row; if you have not seen the representation of a man during the three nights you may believe that you will not be married. Widows can use this power as well as unmarried girls with this difference- that instead of placing the rod under the bed or at the bedside, widows must place the poplar at the foot of the bed.

For Men to Do the Same

The man must take pulverized coral, powdered and mixed with the blood of a white pigeon; he will make a small piece of clay, making it into a human figure, and after having wrapped the same in a piece of blue taffeta, hang it from their necks, and will place under the shroud of the bedside a myrtle branch, and say while laying there the same prayer heretofore marked, changing only the words to *ancillae tuae quem sim nuptura, virum in iis, qui in eorum commodum statutis, servo tuo quam sim nupturus uxorem.*

To Keep Your Man Loyal

Take a goat penis, a wolf penis, and the oil of the wolves eyes, and reduce it all to powder by calcination; have him ingest it in your presence and we can be assured of his loyalty; marrow of the spine from the back of the wolf has the same effect.

To Cause a Girl to Dance Naked

Take wild marjoram, frank marjoram, wild thyme, verbena, the leaves of myrtle, walnut leaves, and three small fennel stems, all gathered on the eve of St. John in June before sunrise. It should be all dried in the shade, powdered, and kept in fine silk cloth. When you wish to utilize the material, blow the powder in the air in the place where the girl will pass by quickly, such that she will breathe it in, or make smoke with it as tobacco is smoked and the same effect will follow. A famous author adds that the effect will be even more potent if this is done in a place where oil lamps are burning nearby.

To Prosper at Gambling

Take a dead eel that was killed by suffocating it on land, take the gall of a bull that has been killed by the fury of the dogs, and put it into the skin of the eel with a dram of vulture blood, linking the eel skin at both ends with string, and put it in a pile of composting manure for the space of a fortnight, and then you will dry this in a heated oven with fern plucked the eve of St. John; then you will make a bracelet from this on which you write with a crow-quill, and in your own blood, these four letters HVTY, and wearing this bracelet around your arm, you will make a fortune in all places of gambling.

To Prosper At Fishing

You should assemble this material in a place where fish are abundant. Take cow blood, black goat blood, the intestinal blood of a sheep, thyme, oregano, flour, marjoram, garlic, wine lees, and the fat or marrow of the same aforesaid animals; mix this all together and you will make small balls from it, throwing them into the waters, and the fishing will be marvelous.

Another Method

Crush nettles with sheets of couch grass, and add as well houseleek to this. Add the juice of boiled corn water, thyme, and marjoram, and put this composition in a net to catch fish, and in a short time the net will be full.

Another Method

Take yeast with cumin, old cheese, wheat flour and good wine lees; grind it all together and compact it into small balls of the size of a pea, then throw these into rivers where there is abundance of fish and the water is calm, and all the fish will become drunk, such that you can take them in by hand, and soon after they will recover from their drunkenness and be as before.

Another Method

Take the marigold flower, with marjoram, wheat flour, old butter, goat fat with earthworms, ground and mixed together and do the same. This attracts many fish.

Another Method

To bring the fish of the sea to one spot, you will take three mussel shells; And having pulled the flesh out of them, you write with your own blood on the shells, the two following words, *JA Sabaoth*; And having thrown these shells in the place where you'll want the fish to assemble, they will appear there quickly.

Another Method

To fish many crayfish, when we have found out where they are present, we will put traps into the water, in which we will have thrown bits of goat casings or some skinned frogs, and by this means we will attract a large number of them.

To Keep Birds Out of Your Crops

Find the largest toad that you can find, and put it into a clay pot along with a bat, and write, inside the pot lid, this word, *Achizech,* with raven blood; bury this pot in the middle of a sown field, and birds will stay away from the field. When the season arrives when the beans begin to mature, must remove the pot and throw it away from the field in some roadworks.

To Hunt Birds Effectively

Take an owl and bind it to a tree in the forest or within a copse, and beside the owl place a large candle, well lit. Then, two or three people will make noise around the tree with drums, and the birds will come in crowds, perching near the owl to make war, and it will be easy to kill as many as desired with firearm or bow.

Another Method

You will soak in water seed grain that serves as food for birds, with a little white hellebore; And those birds who eat these grains will suddenly weaken, such that you can take them by hand.

Another Method

THE PETIT ALBERT

If you want to capture crows and ravens alive, you will make strong paper horns of a blue color, and then you cover the inside with glue, and shall set a piece of stinking meat to attract the crows or ravens, such that upon thrusting their heads into these cones, the glue sticks to them to pluck their feathers, and it will stick to them as a cap that will block their view, when they want to fly, and so they will be easy to take.

Another Method

You can mix nux vomica into bird food, causing the birds to faint, and making them easy to take.

To Prosper At Caring for Birds

If you suspend inside the bird loft, the skull of an old man or milk of a woman who is nursing a child, the pigeons will reproduce profusely, either by foreigners that they will attract or among themselves, and all will live peacefully and without rancor.

Another Method

If you have a large loft where you do have many pigeons, you prepare them the following composition for preventing them from deserting the loft, and instead attract others to it; thirty pounds of millet, three pounds of cumin, five pounds of honey; half a pound of black pepper, two pounds of seed of Chaste Tree. Mix this all using river water until the material is dissolved, and pour it into clay pots and cook it on a cement oven; you will cook this for the space of a half hour on low heat, making a massive amount of bird food. Place this all in the center of your loft, and you will in a short time be compensated for the expense you have made.

Another Method

I read in the writings of an ancient Kabbalist, that to prevent snakes from bothering your birds, write with a mix of blood around the loft and its windows, the word Adam, and you will make also a sweet perfume there or else use coltsfoot: it is believed that a wolf's head hanging on the loft has a similar effect.

Another Method

The old books teach the best practices for raising pigeons well, and experience makes known that we can not give them anything better than fatty dough and fricasseed beans with cumin and honey.

To Prevent Dogs From Becoming Aggressive

To prevent dogs from acting aggressively towards you, wear the dried heart and eyes of a wolf on your body. The great antipathy which is between dog and the wolf causes this effect.

Another Method, to Prevent Rabies

As the bite of a rabid dog is infinitely dangerous, it

is thus good to have quick remedies to defend against the fatal consequences of this malignant bite. So crush laserwort seed sprouts with good vinegar and make a plaster that you apply to the bite wound, and anoint it as well with balsam oil. Fresh wild rose root, being crushed and applied, is, as the words of Pliny suggest, also a speedy remedy against the bite of the rabid dog. Good naturalists assure that taking the beast and burning it to ashes, and drinking good wine in the same setting, provides healing as well. Reduce river crabs to ashes with fire during the summer, in the transit of the moon as a crescent, when the Sun enters the sign of Leo, and powder the burned crabs. We give half a drachma in broth of the same to the patient, evening and morning for fifteen days, and he will heal. Galen ensures that this remedy has never failed him in need. But I suggest that we do not rely so much on any single remedy, for we can do all those little remedies in the way.

To Ward Off Wolves

If you wear on your body the eyes and heart of a dog that died by violence, you will not need to fear wolves, and they will flee like cowardly rabbits. If you hang the tail of a wolf that was killed in a fight in the manger or a big barn or with your sheep, wolves will stay away from them. The same effect happens in a village if you bury some wolf bones under the streets. I read in the writings of one naturalist, a very surprising way to take in large numbers of wolves, even to depopulate an entire country swarming with them; you must obtain a good amount of fish, called biemmi or marine wolf, which are carnivorous, and after having cleaned well the meat and removed the scales, they should be crushed in a mortar with lamb flesh, and then, you will bring this mixture into the woods where the wolves reside. Create a large coal fire to the opposition of the wind; that is to say, the wind must blow into the wolf-infested area, so that the smoke will billow towards the wolves. They will be attracted to the burning bait, consume the fish, and fall into a coma, often dying.

There are so many books that are filled with secrets to destroy pests, and I do not agree that it is necessary to list many here in this book, but these kinds of secrets that have become too common to ignore anyone. So I will move on to the most curious things that will satisfy the reader.

To Prevent Drunkenness

As man has nothing more valuable than his reason, and it becomes absent when too much wine is drunk, it is proper to give him a method to protect against it. When you are invited to a meal where you fear to succumb to the sweet violence of Bacchus, you drink before you sit two table spoons of figwort and a dollop of good olive oil, and you can drink wine safely. You shall observe the glass or cup in which you will be served a drink, do not sate yourself with sweet foods or potato because both of these foods contribute much to drunkenness. If one becomes intoxicated he must, for the man, wrap his genitals in a cloth that is soaked in strong vinegar, and the woman who has succumbed to the intoxication should put a similar cloth on her nipples, and they will come back to their senses.

THE PETIT ALBERT

To Restore Stale Wine

Wine which has become stale may be recovered in the following manner. If it be the harvest season, and the grape begins to mature, you will take approximately half of the large ripe grapes: you will clean a barrel, in which you put two armfuls of chips of good, fresh wood; you water these with the juices of the grapes, and mix this together by hand. Having shut and laid the barrel, leave it for three days. Take the stale wine and the pour it into the wood, and after three days it will have become as fresh wine.

Another Method

You will make an herbal decoction; namely, a handful of each of the following: marjoram, thyme, laurel, myrtle, juniper berry, lemon peels peels of orange; you should boil it in twenty quarts of water until the it is reduced to fifteen quarts or roughly the amount needed for whatever barrel you are using. To refresh the wine, you will wash said barrel with the boiling decoction, and let the material soak in; then add two armfuls of wood chips to the brew in the barrel. You will drawshot of the wine, then leave it to rest for eight days on the grated chips, and it will be even fresher than it was when it was first made.

Another Method

I learned from the butler of a German prince this method: Dry in the oven fifty clusters of good grapes and a half bushel of sweet almond shells, ensure that these shells are slightly browned, as they accommodate themselves to the oven. Whisk twelve egg whites into the mix thoroughly and pour them into the barrel where the spoiled wine is. Now put in the almond shells and the hot grapes, and let stand eight days, and you will have beautiful and good wine. When wine becomes sour, it may also be restored with corn which is cooked until it bursts, adding one hundredth quantity of the same to the barrel, by volume.

To Make Excellent Vinegar

Obtain a good wine box, in which you will put sweet peppers and rye bread with a sour leaven: make sure it's fresh and has not laid in the sun too long. We can do without wine vinegar in this way: take a load of wild pears, mash them well, and let this ferment for three days in a barrel, and then, for thirty days, you water them in two jars of water per day, water in which you boiled the peppers with ginger; after thirty days you will press the mashed pears, and you will have good vinegar.

Making Good Liquers

To make good Greek wine, supplying many drinks. Mix the following decoction: six pounds of good sugar, ginger, galanga, the grains of paradise, cloves, four ounces each, with two lemon peels; you will boil it all in six quarts of spring water, reducing the material by half, and after filtering the same, lay it in the barrel and you'll have made excellent Greek wine. For a muscat wine, you take licorice, fern, anise, nutmeg, and calamus, each two drachmas in weight, and grind all this together lightly, and place the brew in its barrel, and the barrel in a white bag, so that the bag can be up to half of theis halfway up the barrel for ten or twelve days, and you will have good Muscat wine. Due to the materials used above, the barrel must be retired after three years. The wine ought to be drunk quickly, or can be stored in its hogshead for three years, and to preserve the same, you will put the following composition in as well: you will take four pounds of good natural honey, a dram of powdered cloves, and the same amount of ginger and mace, with four pints of spring water; you will boil it all together for two hours, and you will take care to skim it perfectly; strain this through a cloth, removing the clove and mace. And when this composition is complete, fill the barrel halfway with it and it will make the bad barrel good again. If you want to make exquisite wine, you will take one drachma of musk and one of aloe wood, with two drams of cinnamon, cloves, and grains of paradise, with two pounds of sugar; good for the amount of one hundred drinks; all boiled in four quarts of water.

An Excellent And Fast Hippocras

For four pints of wine hippocras, you will prepare the materials that follow; a good book of fine sugar, two ounces of cinnamon coarsely crushed, an ounce of paradise seed, an ounce of cardamom, and two grains of ambergris, and crushed candy sugar; you will make these all into a clear syrup, you purify the same by passing two or three times through a cheesecloth, and then mix the syrup with four pints of excellent wine, and you'll have the best hippocras that can be made.

THE PETIT ALBERT

The True Water of Armenia

You will take six pounds of the finest morello cherries you may have. After having removed the stem and the pit, cook them at the stove in a clear bowl with a quart of spring water and make a strong boil for hours. Then you will put them through a cheesecloth, crushing them and obtaining the juice. Now make a syrup, with three pounds of fine sugar, four ounces of cinnamon, an ounce of cloves, a good ounce of nutmeg, one ounce of grains of paradise, an ounce of cardamom, four grains of musk, ambergris finely ground in a mortar with candy sugar, all lightly crushed together. When the syrup is done and well clarified, you'll mix it with four pints of good wine in a large jar, shaken together well, and laid in the sun for two weeks and you will have excellent wine spirit. The grounds which remain behind may be taken and used to make a more common hippocras by the same method before.

Growing Sweet Melons

Obtain any species of sweet melon seed, and let it steep for two days in a syrup which will consist of raspberries, cinnamon, cardamom, two grains of musk and ambergris finely ground. The syrup must not be thick and warm when you put it in the seed infusion; now sow it over a layer of horse manure, and have great care not to overwater the points and hope to avoid also the excessive rains. If done properly, this yields melons fit for royalty.

Growing Good Grapes

THE PETIT ALBERT

You have to have a cherry tree that is planted against a wall or trellis, with good sun exposure and good soil, and have a skilled gardener plant a couple of good vine stocks on said cherry tree, doing so in spring or late winter. Spare no good manure or watering and the grapes will be marvelous when they are mature.

To Prosper At Growing Wheat

You will need a pound of salts, composed of sulfur, nitre, and saltpeter. Good druggists have this salt. Place this in six quarts of boiling water with two new books of good wheat seed, until the wheat seed begins to shrink and die, and then you will pass this composition through clear water; after this you will infuse into the cooled mix as much as you can of good wheat seed for twenty-four hours, your field already prepared. Sow this wheat seed thus infused and having dried the composition. Til and furrow the land and you will see by experience that the wheat you'll have sown will produce twenty times more than common wheat: it is true that we should not do that twice in the same land; because it will destroy the soil.

To Prevent Animals From Destroying Your Crops

You will need ten large crayfish, which you put in a vessel filled with water, and expose them to the sun for ten days. Now broadcast the water for eight days while sowing; and when it is done yousprinkle whatever is left, and you will see that the fields are clean of rats and other pests.

To Divine Whether Next Year's Planting Will Be Good

THE PETIT ALBERT

Zoroaster himself gives an infallible secret to know the abundance of the harvest for the following year. It takes about two days, in June, to perform. Prepare a small dirt patch, like we ordinarily ready to be planted: you will sow all manner of seed in this, and because that in this season heat is hot and could affect what seeds are sown and which are more convenient to sow as well. After that you will see which seeds thrive and which do not, and will see which have the best appearance in time as the heat begins to reign over the horizon; as you will be notified by this test which seeds prosper and which die or produce little. So the wise farmer will take it on its measures for an abundant harvest.

Another Method

You shall see in the spring in what state the walnuts are: for if they appear loaded with foliage and few flowers, rest assured that nature will be stingy in the distribution of its wealth; if instead you see abundance of flowers on the nut trees, and the amount exceeds that of the leaves, fertility is assured: the almond tree performs similarly.

To Defend Against Illness

Foul smells are naturally contrary to the human health and the stench is sometimes fatal, as Fioraventus wrote, who says that if you take the filth of human blood and phlegmatic fluids well dried up, if it is mixed with styrax and these are burned in a room, the stench will be fatal. To be protected against these deadly infections, I will propose a sovereign antidote which will triumph over all kinds of venoms and poisons.

THE PETIT ALBERT

You will take in the growing season the leaves of hypericum, before it casts its flower as much as you are able to hold in your hands. Put them in the sun with four pounds of olive oil for ten days and then will expose them on the stove in a water bath, in hot water, and then you will press the juice out of the leaves, and will put it in a vessel or bottle or strong glass jar and when the wort is flowered and seed, you will put a handful of that seed and the flowers in the jar as well and will boil it all on the fire in a water bath for one hour. Then you will add thirty scorpions, a serpent, and a green frog, you shall cut off their heads and feet, and after a bit, boil it also. You will put two ounces of each herb following in thereafter; crushed gentian root, white dictamum, the root of the tormentil, rhubarb, the Armenian bole, thus prepared. The ointment ought to be green in color. All this will be exposed to the sun during the scorching days of midsummer, after having well sealed the jar, and finally you must deposit the jar for three months in composting manure. And after that time you will remove the jar from the manure, and keep the treasure in a vase of tin or strong glass to use it. The usage is to rub around the heart, the temples, the nostrils, the sides and along the spine, and you will feel that this is an antidote against all kinds of poisons. It is also good to cure the bites of venomous beasts.

Ancient Talismans and the Usage Thereof

The great reputation Paracelsus has gained in the world by the deep science of his works gives much authority to this writing. It provides, as an indubitable thing, that if we form talismans according to the method he gives, they will produce effects that will surprise those who will experience them. This is what I experienced myself with admiration; a very happy and successful life. Here in what way he speaks in his magical archidoxis.

Nobody can, without temerity, cast doubt that the stars and celestial planets have the most dominant influences on everything that is in this lower world; for since we see and that we essentially feel that domination the planets, their influences on man, who is the image of God and has the advantage of reason; how much more so should we believe that they dominate and affect metals, stones, and whatever nature and art can produce; since all these things are lower than man, and more capable of receiving, without resistance, their influences since they are deprived of reason and free will, and that man has the advantage that he is able to use these material things, for it to attract the influences of the stars?

But what is worthy of being known and well noticed is that the seven planets in the cosmos never influence more effectively than through the seven metals of their own nature, that is to say, which have sympathy with their substance. About this the wise Kabbalists that experienced by the sublime penetration of their sciences, what are the specific metals to planets, they determined gold for the Sun, the day of Sunday, argentum to the Moon, to Monday, iron to Mars, to Tuesday, the quicksilver for Mercury, to Wednesday, tin to Jupiter, to Thursday, copper to Venus, to Friday, and lead to Saturn, the Saturday. On this basis, we give here the way of making talismans, which the ancient sages referred to as the seals of the planets.

THE PETIT ALBERT

Talisman Of the Sun For Sunday

```
 6 32 13  3 33 23
 7 31 27 28 28 30
19 14 16 15 23 24
18 20 22 21 17 13
32 22 10 19 26 12
36 15 15 14 18 13
```

This talisman must be composed with the most exquisite and purest of gold, which is that of Arabia or of Hungary. Here it is formed into a round plate, well polished on both sides; and upon one of these sides we draw a square composed of six lines of numbers that thus progress from one corner to another, shaped into the semblance of St. Andrew's cross. There are one hundred and eleven. And

THE PETIT ALBERT

that is mysterious as well, and all be informed is that the numbers which will be marked in all talismans or seals of the planets are large numbers of stars that are under the control of each planet, and they lord over their attributes as their subjects, and this is why those who are versed in astrology, called precursors planets or stars premieres, and they are confluent and present, they have others under their direction, for the distribution of their influences. On the other side of the plate, you have to brand the hieroglyphic figure of the planet, which is crowned king in his royal throne, holding in his right hand a scepter on the head with the Sunwith the sun on his head and the name of Jupiter, and brandishing his scepter with a roaring lion at his feet. And so that this operation is done accurately and in suitable circumstances, you will burn with two very clean irons everything I said above, not to lose the favorable moment of the constellation, because it is necessary that printing is done at the time we have observed that the sun will be in conjunction with the moon in the first degree of Leo; And when the gold plate will be marked on both sides with the above irons, you promptly wrap the same in a thin cloth. What to say just the two engraved irons, must likewise agree to the making of talismans of other planets; printing must be done in the favorable moment of the constellation; because you must know that it is in this moment that the planet spreads and likewise prints its benign influences on the talisman; a supernatural way and the whole mystery. The properties of this talisman of the sun are that the person who will wear it with confidence and reverence, will become pleasant to the powers of the earth, kings, princes, the nobles which we want to develop kindness, we will abound in wealth and in honor, and we will be honored by

THE PETIT ALBERT

all the world.

Talisman Of the Moon For Monday

```
37 78 29 70 21 62 13 45  5
 6 38 79 30 71 22 63 14 46
47  7 59 80 31 72 23 55 15
16 48  8 40 81 32 64 24 56
57 17 49  9 41 73 33 65 25
26 58 18 50  1 42 74 34 66
67 27 59 19 51  2 43 75 35
35 68 19 60 11 52  3 44 76
77 28 69 20 61 12 53  4 45
```

This talisman must be composed with the most pure silver that we can find, which we will make into a round plate, well polished; On the front side we engrave nine lines of numbers, each of which will contain the mysterious number of three hundred sixty nine, as shown below in the next square. On the other side of the plate, must be printed the hieroglyphic image of the planet, to be a woman covered with a large and wide dress with both feet on the ground, branches in her right hand, and a star of great brilliance upon her head with the word, moon. The operation must be performed on a Monday of spring, when we will have the first degree of Capricorn or Virgo in favorable aspect to Jupiter or Venus. Wrap the talisman in a white cloth; and it will be greatly useful to destroy diseases; it will preserve travelers from harm and ward off thieves; it will cause laborers to be favorable to merchants.

Talisman Of Mars For Tuesday

This talisman must be formed on a polished and round plate, of the best iron. The mysterious numbers will be sixty five. And on the other side of the plate will be formed the hieroglyphic figure of the face of the planet, representing a soldier, holding in his left hand a shield, and the right a sword, having a star on his head, with the name

THE PETIT ALBERT

of Mars.

```
14 10  5 12 18
20 12  6 32 24
21 27 14  9 15
22 13 19 15 26
23  1 20 16 18
```

The printing instruments must be made of finely tempered steel, and the printing is done in the time we have observed that the Moon is a benign and favorable appearance with some other planet, between the first degree of the sign of Aries or Sagittarius; and It will even be good as talisman plate is put at the burning furnace, to blast the plate in a furnace before printing to make it more suitable for receiving the etching of mysterious figures. When it is cooled, wrap it in a piece of red taffeta. This talisman will have the property of rendering invulnerable those that perform the will of the cosmos reverently; give him power and an extraordinary force; he will win his battles. The planet Mars affects so marvelously on this talisman, when it is done accurately, that if it is buried in the foundations of a fortress, it becomes impregnable, and those who want to undertake the attack, are destroyed. And if it is formed when the constellation of Mars is in opposition to the retrograde planets favorability, it will bring bad luck wherever it is put, and there cause dissensions, rebellions,

THE PETIT ALBERT

and civil war; I know that a great statesman wore a similar talisman in England, in the time of the revolution of Cromwell.

Talisman Of Mercury For Wednesday

This talisman must be formed on a round plate of fixed mercury, (I will give below the way to fix mercury for talismans, as I have done this myself.) When the plate is made and polished it is printed with the irons on one side, with the mysterious number of two hundred and sixty, distributed in eight lines, as seen here represented.

And on the other side of the plate is the hieroglyphic figure of the planet Mercury, representing an angel with wings on her back and its heels, holding in its right hand a caduceus shaped scepter, and a star on its head, with the name of Mercury. Print the talisman in a favorable time of the constellation, as will be observed before starting the business. And when it is completed, wrap the talisman

THE PETIT ALBERT

in a cloth of purple colored silk.

```
 8   8 59 43  4 64 63 11
49 16 14 52 52 14 10 56
41 43 22 24 34 29 18 49
32 34 35 29 29 38 39 24
40 32 27 37 30 30 31 33
17 47 46 21 20 43 42 24
 9  55 54 12 13 51 50 16
64 12  3  12 50  6 77 57
```

    This talisman will have the property of making the bearer eloquent and give them great stealth, and and will aid them in studying the sciences. If the talisman is placed in your wine for only an hour, it makes the memory so happy that it may recall everything with ease; it can even cure all kinds of fevers. If you put it under the head of the bed, it provides prophetic, lucid dreams.

THE PETIT ALBERT

Talisman Of Jupiter For Thursday

```
16  3  2 13
15 15  1  3
 9  6  7 12
 4 14 14  2
```

This talisman must be formed on a round plate, made from the purest tin. Print on one side of the mysterious number of the planet, which is thirty four distributed in four lines, as we see here. And on the other side of the plate is printed the hieroglyphic figure of the face of the planet, to be a man dressed in robes, holding in his hands a book, which he seems to read, and above his head a shining star, with this word; Jupiter. Begin printing the mysterious figures on the plate, with irons, when you shall observe that the constellation of the planet will be favorable, when the moon enters the first degree of Libra, with Jupiter in good aspect with the sun. When the operation is finished, you will wrap the talisman in a piece of blue silk. This talisman will give to those who will carry it reverently the love and support of those which they wish it from. The bearer will continually gain more wealth. It will make the bearer fortunate in trading, commerce, and in all enterprises; it dissipates sorrows, cares, and unwelcome challenges.

Talisman Of Venus For Friday

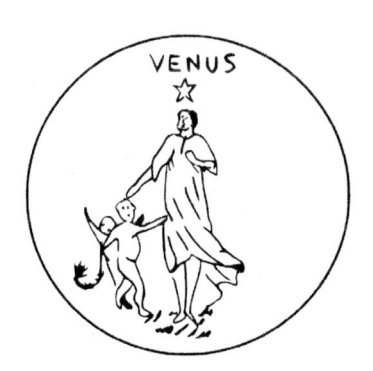

This talisman must be formed on a round copper plate well purified and polished. Print on one side of the mysterious number five hundred and seventy, distributed in seven lines, as marked here.

THE PETIT ALBERT

And on the other side of the plate is the hieroglyphic figure of the face of the planet, which is to be a woman lasciviously dressed, having close to his right thigh a cherubim holding a bow and a fiery arrow, and the woman holds in her left hand a musical instrument, like a guitar, and above its head a shining star, with this word, Venus. Printing will be done with the irons, in the moment that the constellation of Venus will be in good aspect with some favorable planet, the Moon being in in the first degree of Taurus or Virgo. The operation being finished, the talisman must be wrapped in green silk. And he who will wear this talisman can ensure the good graces of those that he desires, and to be loved passionately, both by women and men. It also has the virtue of reconciling foes, causing them to cease fighting and drink together, such that they become friends; it also makes the wearer talented at playing all manner of music.

```
22 47 16 41 10 35  4
25 23 48 17 42 11  9
30  6 24 49 18 36 12
13 31  7 25 43 19 37
30 14 32  1 26 44 20
21 39  8 32  2 17 45
46 15 40  9 35  3 27
```

THE PETIT ALBERT

Talisman Of Saturn For Saturday

This talisman must be formed on a round plate, out of the purest lead, and you will print on the front side, this mysterious number, distributed in fifteen lines, following the layout shown here.

```
249
753
618
```

And on the other side of the plate, will be put the

hieroglyphic figure of the face of the planet, which will be a bearded old man, holding in his hand a kind of pickaxe, hunched over somewhat, and above his head will be a star with the word, Saturn. You will start printing the mysterious figures with your irons when you have observed that Saturn is in a constellation of favorable aspect, the moon entering the first degree with the sign of Taurus or Capricorn. And when the operation is over, you must wrap the talisman in a black silk fabric piece.

This talisman is of great help, first, for women who are in search of childbirth because they are suffering almost no pain from the same; multiple individuals have tested this manner of the talisman. It also multiplies and increases the things with which it is placed- If a rider carries the talisman in his left boot, his horse will not be injured in any way. It has all the effects contrary to these, when it is formed in the time that the constellation of Saturn is in a disastrous situation and a retrograde moon is in the above signs.

Forming Plaques For the Talismans, In Mercury

You have to choose a Wednesday in Springtime, when Mercury's constellation is on either side with the sun and Venus, and after invoking the spirit of Mercury controlling this planet, prepare the necessary materials, in the following manner: sal ammoniac, verdegris, Roman vitriol, two ounces of each well pulverized. Put it all together in an iron pot, with three quarts of water, and heat it so that everything boils up reducing down to a pint of liquid, and then add two ounces of mercury, and stir it well with a spoon until they become thick and homogenized;

THE PETIT ALBERT

then let them cool, and subsqeuently filter the liquid out. At the bottom, a bit of gray sediment will remain, which you must wash with water, two or three times, always filtering out the liquid each time, and then spread the paste on a flat, polished wooden plank, allowing the sun to dry the same. After this add two ounces of good earth, and much Senna powder, and put it all in a sealed crucible luted with another crucible ensortesuch that both when placed together end to end make a single vessel without an opening, and so that nothing can evaporate when the vessels are heated. These crucibles must be sealed together with a loam paste of horse dung and iron filings. Do not put the luted crucible in the furnace, but rather a simple stove, and make sure the vessels are completely dry before you begin this work. When the crucible has been cooking for one hour, increase the heat until the vessels begin to change color. At the third hour the fire will be increased again, and you must continuously feed the fire with bellows, then leave the crucible to cool. The material will have collected at the bottom of the lower vessel, in small grains, and you must take these grains, mix them with borax, and place them in a new vessel; this being done you will have a very fine fixed, granulated mercury, clean and pure for forming talismans or mysterious rings that have the property of attracting the benign influences of the planet Mercury, provided that your work is correct according to the rules of art.

Formulating Talismans Used by Other Kabbalists

You will use the same metal plates which were spoken of before. Start the operation at such hours and appropriate moments to attract the benign influences of the celestial forces spoken of for each; on one side of the plate is printed, squarely shaped, characters that are marked below; that is to say, for the Sun, those that are found in the first line. For the Moon, those that are found in the second line. For Mars, those we find in the third line. For Mercury, those, which can be found on the fourth line. For Jupiter, those we find in the fifth line. For Venus, those we found in the sixth line. For Saturn, those we find in the seventh line. You can engrave the other side of the plate with the same figures spoken of before, and you will experience wonderful effects. I have no doubt that, if that book falls from my hands into those of people of small minds, being ignorant, they will become superstitious; because they will imagine that the admirable wonders I treat of here are made by the ministry of evil spirits; for, they say, how can we understand that a metal plate, in charge of some characters and figure, operates things that surpass the ordinary forces of nature? I refute these kinds of people and say thus: So you believe that evil spirits can do those things which surpass the usual order of nature? But why, then, do not you think the creator of the universe is powerful enough to be imprinted upon all of nature itself? Why do you not instead acknowledge that he who gave our race the secret to attract to itself under a heavy mass of iron, such forces, from the celestial regions to the earthly, is powerful enough to give force to the stars, which are creatures infinitely more perfect than humans, and also those which are even more precious, upon the earth? These have properties and secrets of virtues, which surpass the reach of our minds, especially as these stars are governed by heavenly intelligences which regulate their movements.

THE PETIT ALBERT

But how difficult can it be to believe that from characters or certain numbers on a metal plate, can be produced many wonders, since it is believed that one can obviously see that in some small parts of spherical materials, triangular rows come from the same in a certain order, produce admirable effects, not only to attract a mass of iron, but always turn the needle compasses in the direction of the North Star, and adjust the dials to the sun, and such.

I wish I was able to ask these unscrupulous people, why in Switzerland to even today, where there are many snakes, because of the mountains, why do these snakes fear the following in Greek, and if they hear the three words "osy, osya, osy" they quickly clog one of their ears with the tip of their tail and flatten themselves sideways against the ground, so as not to hear these words, such that they are unable to bring harm to people? If I am told that it is nature that produces this instinct in them, why would nature be less ingenious in other creatures?

Salamanders, Gnomes, Nymphs, and Sylphs

I will turn perhaps many people against me if I say that there are creatures in the four elements that are neither pure animals or men, although they have the capability of reason without having a true soul. The famous Paracelsus speaks even more clearly, saying that these people are not the elements of the lineage of Adam, although they appear to be genuine men, but they are instead species of creatures, always different from ours. Porphyry mentioning Paracelsus, said that not only are these creatures reasonable, but even are able to love and serve God through worship; and as proof of his words, he speaks of a sublime oration here, and very mysterious are those creatures that live in the element of fire, as the Salamanders do; maybe I will ask my readers to speak on this subject, which may be useful should another such book as this be made.

Oration Of the Salamanders

Ethereennes, ruler of the countryside, where sits the throne of your power, from the pinnacle of which thy terrible eyes see all, and your holy ears hear all. Hear thy children, whom thou hast loved from birth long ago; for thy great and eternal life and majesty shine the stars above this world. You are high above them all, oh glittering fire, and thou hold council with thyself by your own splendor, and from your essence come inexhaustible streams of lights that feed your infinite mind. That spirit produces all things, and makes this an inexhaustible treasure of matter, which cannot fail the living generation because of the countless forms with which the world is pregnant, and which you have filled in the beginning.

In this spirit also originate those most holy kings who are standing around thy throne, and who compose thy court, oh universal father, singular and immortal father blessed by all mortals! You created things and beings which are wonderfully similar to thy eternal thought and thy adorable essence. Thou hast set above us all the angels which announce to the world your will. Finally, you create a third kind of rulers in the four elements. Our continual exercise is to praise and worship you in your desires. We burn with the desire to possess you. Oh father! Oh mother, the most tender of mothers! Oh admirable example of the emotion and tenderness of mothers. Oh son, the flower of every son! Oh form of all forms! Soul, spirit, harmony and number of all things, keeps us and we shall be propitious. Amen.

All of the ancient philosophers from many centuries past, who were convinced that the four elements are inhabited by rational creatures, categorize them in this following way: The element of fire is inhabited by Salamanders; the element of air is inhabited by sylphs; the element of water is inhabited by nymphs; and the element of earth is inhabited by gnomes. And they believe that these creatures were made by the Creator, to render important services to men, and punish them when they are disobedient to his will.

It is claimed that these extraordinary creatures are of a spiritual nature; not a spirituality which excludes matter, but a spirituality that does not allow for physicality, a matter extending beyond the physical, and as imperceptible as the air; On this principle, the wise Kabbalists who knew the nature of these elemental creatures, said they had other qualities of movement and power; such that in a moment they can come from afar to the rescue of people who need their ministry, and can penetrate any area where these same men are being held.

In regard their morals, these beings are very lawful, according to the same laws of nature, and they are great enemies of those men which live in licentiousness and

THE PETIT ALBERT

against the light of reason. And it is on this principle that the wise Kabbalists, who gave many signs and symbols to achieve discovery of the mysteries of occultism, have recommended over all things to the followers of this sublime science, virtue in good men, freedom from any impurity, debauchery, or deviation from order and holiness, especially as the greatest marvels that rely on occult science rely upon the ministry of the elementary peoples who are like channels, or rather, the saving influences of benign stars.

In past centuries, when men were of greater moderation of the passions, and had less corruption of nature, these elementary peoples had much attendance with men, far more than in the last few centuries, and one saw their wonders regularly, which brought much admiration, because they seemed to exceed the natural order; but if the corruption of nature reigns, ignorance becomes so great that most men attribute these forces to magic or devilry, almost everything that was carried on by the ministry of the elementary peoples; this is what we can see in the reign of Charlemagne, and in the orders that were made in the reign of Pepin, and the wonders which are mentioned in stories from ancient times; these now pass for fairy tales. I refer to the writings of Paracelsus for the more learned of my readers who want to be taught more thoroughly of these elementary peoples, and their secret influences, which they have with men. Those who have traveled in the northern countries, and above all in Lapland, can not ignore the fact that Gnomes inhabit these regions, to guarantee safety, warning the people when they work. They help the land and make the people acquainted with the places where mines are more abundant in precious metals.

The Lapps are so much accustomed to the frequent appearances of Gnomes, such that, far from being frightened, they are saddened when they do not appear when they are working in the mines; because it is a sign that these mines are filled with impure ores, when there are no gnomes therein. It is a popular claim that the creator has committed gnomes to guard subterranean wealth, and they have the ability to deliver the same wealth as they see fit.

Those who are engaged in the discovery of gold and silver mines, observe some ceremonies to conciliate the good will of the Gnomes, so that they do not contradict them in their businesses. Experience has taught them that the gnomes like strong perfumes, and that's why the wise Kabbalists ordered the people to burn the same each day, in accordance with planetary cycles. And as I know from experience that many people have managed to discover the treasures, through perfumes, I will, for my readers, give here the true way of doing so that they may be pleasing to the gnomes which guard these same deposits of wealth. You must know that of all the creatures that live in the four elements, there are none that are more inclined to harm or do good to men, according to the subjects they are given.

Perfume For Sunday And the Sun

All perfumes must be made in a small stove, with charcoal made from hazel or laurel wood. To burn the incense, it must be on a new fire that is sparked by stone alone; it is good to observe that the same stone, the wick,

THE PETIT ALBERT

the match and the candle are new rather than formerly used, and they must have served no profane use as gnomes are easily angered. The fragrance of Sunday is composed of the following. Namely, the fourth part of an ounce of saffron, as much aloe wood, as much of balsam, as much of laurel seed, as much of cloves, the same amount of myrtle, the same amount of incense base, and a grain each of musk and ambergris. This must be pulverized and mixed together, and you will form the mix into small grains with a little tragacanth gum, soaked in rose water, and when they are completely dry, you will use it on occasion by throwing three of the said grains onto hot coals.

Perfume For Monday And the Moon

This perfume must be composed of the following. You will take a green frog head, the eyes of a white bull, white poppy seeds, pure storax, frankincense, benzoin resin, and a little camphor, which shall be pulverized and mixed. Form a paste of the same with the blood of a young goose or a turtledove, and this paste you will form into small grains for you to use as before when they have dried, adding three grains only to your coals.

Perfume For Tuesday And Mars

This perfume must be composed of euphorbia, of bdellium, sal ammoniac, hellebore root, powdered magnetite, and a bit of yellow sulfur. Pulverize and mix it well, and make a paste with black cat blood and the macerated brains of the raven mixed with the same, and this paste you will form into grains and use as before.

THE PETIT ALBERT

Perfume For Wednesday And Mercury

This perfume must be composed of ash seed, aloe wood, good storax, benzoin, azure powder, and peacock feather tips. Pulverize and mix this all together with the blood of a swallow and a little macerated deer brain, you will make a paste, and this paste you will form into small grains, used as before.

Perfume For Friday And Venus

This perfume must be comprised of musk, ambergris, aloe wood, dried roses, and red coral. The material must be first soaked with pure water, then pulverized and mixed with the blood of pigeon or dove, and the brains of two or three sparrows. Form, dry, and use as before.

Perfume For Saturday And Saturn

This perfume must be composed of black poppy seed, seed of henbane, mandrake root powder, and some good myrtle. Pulverize and mix the materials, then add bat blood and the brains of a black cat. You will make a paste thereof, and form its grains, drying it and using it as before.

We said before that the gnomes will respond to these scents. As Gnomes are, such are all creatures that inhabit the four elements, all of which may choose to do good or harm humans, according to the actions of the same humans; that is why those who work at mining in search of

THE PETIT ALBERT

treasures, being warned of the presence of such beings, do everything they can to make them comfortable, and take precautions as they can against their anger. Experience has made known several times that verbena and laurel are of good use to prevent the Gnomesfrom attacking the works of those who are busy looking for underground treasures. Here we see how Jamblic and the Arbatel speak in their Kabbalistic secrets.

When by natural or supernatural clues, that is to say, by a revelation in your dreams, you will be well assured of where there will be a treasure, you will scent the place with the perfume made for the day you wish to begin such work. Then you must hold in your right hand a branch of green laurel branch, and in your left hand a branch of vervain, and you will make the opening of the land between these two branches. When you have dug out a section equivalent to the height of a man, you will make a crown of these two branches which should be twined around your hat or head, and over that crown you will attach the talisman which is shown here.

Form the talisman upon a plate of pure tin, during the day, being sure that Jupiter is in a positive aspect, with clear skies. Upon one side of the talisman, there will be the figure of fortune, as it is represented here, and across the talisman's face, these words in big character:

And if one is to work several days before arriving at the spot where the treasure is located, the perfume ought to be used each of these days, making sure to use the proper scents. These precautions will cause the Gnomes, the

THE PETIT ALBERT

guardians of treasure, to avoid confrontation with you, and they may even help you in your business. I have seen this myself firsthand, witnessing the happy success at the same in the old castle at Orvieto.

I have spoken heretofore natural forces which are able to be experimented upon, and the treasure guarded thereof. This now requires further explanation. Paracelsus, in his treatise on occult philosophy, page 489, claims that to find where there are treasures and hidden riches, observe where, at night, specters or ghosts appear among other extraordinary things that scare people which pass through and those who live in these places, and particularly the nights of Friday to Saturday. If one sees spirit lights, strange noises, or various other similar things, we can form a reasonable conjecture that there is in these places some hidden treasure.

But the wise man does not stop at this; we must reason and use our minds to determine the reports of others and their validity, and above all hysterical females who, on chimerical visions, commit honest people to unnecessary searching for such things. Rather it is better to investigate the testimony of people which are not subject to suspicion at all, that is to say, which have probity, and who are a strong mind, and it can be even experimenting on yourself with these kinds of visions, making residence on the premises.

Superstition must not, however, absolutely put off others to all such reports, but rather to carefully examine the circumstances. I am a witness of this- If you wanted to

THE PETIT ALBERT

disbelieve Philip of Ortano, chief surgeon of the regulars at that old castle at Orvieto, one would have overlooked now that success was had and celebration thereafter; for while was a great talker, and persuasive enough in what he said, he drew ridicule because of his rowdy gatherings that several domestic servants and soldiers had had in the place where the treasure was found.

Whoever would attempt to find hidden treasure, should examine the quality of the place, not by the present situation of this place, but compared to what the old stories of the same say; because it should be noted that there are two kinds of hidden treasures. The first kind is gold and silver, which was formed in the bowels of the earth, by the metal under the stars and of the ground where it is. The second kind is gold and silver or coinage, rather, created by a smith, and which has been deposited in the ground for various reasons, such as wars, plagues, and others. That's what the wise treasure hunter must examine, in considering whether those circumstances are suitable to which the stories refer. These kinds of treasures of gold, of coined money, crockery and smithed goods, is usually found in the debris of the old hovels and quality houses and castles, or near ruined old churches or chapels. And Gnomes do not take possession of these kinds of treasures, except in the case where the treasure has been explicitly committed to their care, with the same invited by the use of perfume and talisman. In this conjecture, we must refer to how to dispossess them of such treasure, by stronger perfumes and talismans, as we said; those we form sponsored by the moon and Saturn, the moon entering the signs of Taurus, Capricorn or Virgo, are most effective.

We must, above all, see that those who are engaged in this research will not be easily startled, because gnomes guard treasure commonly, not rarely, fascinating the imagination of workers, creating strange sights and hideous visions; but they are good people as the stories of the past say, and to say that they strangle or kill those who approach the treasures that are in their custody, is madness. If someone has died in the caves, it will rather be because they got lost, or by the infection of these places, or carelessness of workers, or a cave-in because of poor structural support.

Rather, when such horrific things are seen or heard it is a clue that we must dig with even more fervor, for treasure is thus near. You will not draw the ire of the gnomes by speaking of improper things, or by singing, although some things indeed may infuriate them and must be avoided.

If, by advancing the mining, more noise than before

THE PETIT ALBERT

is heard, do not fear, but merely burn more perfume. If someone from the company recites aloudthe oration of the Salamanders which I gave heretofore, this will prevent any harm from these beings. Lord we must vigorously strengthen the work: I say nothing that has not been tested successfully in my presence; the little book of the Enchiridion is good on these occasions, and because of its mysterious prayers.

We must say that transmuted Gnomes have precious metals, vile metals, and other materials, and deceived the ignorant who were not informed of their subtleties: but the wise and prudent miner, who finds in the bowels of the earth these kinds of materials, that naturally shouldn't even be where they are, and who kindles a fire to burn laurel, fern, and verbena, performs a spell which dissipates through the mine and results in the purification of the lesser metals. A fairly common sign of these fantastic transmutations is when we find these vile and sordid materials in vessels, or clay, or carved stone, or bronze; We should not neglect them, but rather heat them and purify them through this means.

I will end on this matter with the secret Cardan gives to find if the treasure is in a place where tunnels are being excavated. He says that one must obtain a large candle, composed of human tallow, and it is enclosed in a piece of witch hazel, made in the manner which is shown in the following way. If the candle being lit in the cave makes a lot of noise and sparkles brightly, it is a sign that there is a treasure in that place, and the closer one approaches the treasure, the more candlelight the candle will produce, and then it will go out when it is right next to it. Other lanterns, thus, would need to be present, for when the candle goes out. When there is reason to believe that spirits are guarding the treasure, it is good to have blessed candles instead of common candles, and ward off the spirits thereby, telling the spirits you will help them find rest if possible, and one must never fail, once having said thus, to follow through.

Fake Mandrakes

There are people who abuse the credulity and simplicity of good folk, which use trickery to profit, or which do the same with certain lesser supernatural forces: One of these is the artificial mandrake, with which they debase the divine oracles. As I passed by Lille in Flanders, I was invited by one of my friends to accompany her to an old woman who spoke of the future, and who passed for a great soothsayer, and I discovered her deceit, which could not be hid a long time as it was fairly crude. This old woman led us into a small dark room, lit only by a lamp, the light which one saw rested on a table covered with a cloth, upon which was a kind of small doll sitting on a tripod, with one arm extended holding in the same left hand a small string of strong untied silk, after which beside it was a small polished iron rod, and below there were a glass of fern, and there was a fly in the glass, which stood approximately the height of two fingers. The trick was that the old woman commanded the mandrake to strike the glass with its rod to answer questions, when really it was just the fly doing so.

THE PETIT ALBERT

The old fraud, for example, said: "I command thee, mandrake, on behalf of the one to whom you must obey, that if Mr. So should have a good trip, hit the rod three times against the glass."

Natural Processes Of Interest

Here is the way to make a candle, which will make the bearer seem to be headless. You will take a snake skin which was recently shed, Greek pitch, virgin wax, and the blood of an ass; then you must mix them all, and cook them with small fire, boiled for three or four hours in an iron pot full of water and then allowed to cool. You will separate the sediment with more water, and you will form this into a candle; the candle must be stored and held within a burial cloth. Anyone who bears this candle when it is lit will seem headless.

On the Same Subject

If you want all those who are in a room to appear in the form of elephants or horses, you will make a perfume in this way. Crush Alkekengi husk with dolphin fat, and form the same into grains, the size of lemon seeds; mix this with the dung of a young cow and then dry this mix well, such that it is able to be cooked upon coals such that the scent shall be released properly, and you'll get the entertainment you want, as long as the room is tightly shut up, so that the smoke can not get out through the door

On the Same Subject

THE PETIT ALBERT

To cause a room to appear filled with snakes and other terrifying images, you must burn the following within a lamp.

Take the fat of a black snake, with its last shed snake skin- you will boil these with verbena in a cauldron where you will put two pots of forge water, and after a quarter of an hour you will take the cauldron off the fire, and place this composition in a piece of burial cloth to dry and cool. Make sure to skim off the fat which lines the water's surface upon cooling. then you will make a candle with the burial shroud of a deceased male, preferably your own son. And having put in the bottom of the lamp the boiled skin of the snake, as a wick, you will fill the lamp with the fat; and when the lamp is turned on with oil of amber, you and all others will see this strange sight, whenever the lamp is burned, and it will confuse those which do not know its secrets.

On the Same Subject

THE PETIT ALBERT

I felt in Flanders the effect of a lamp which can cause a plague of frogs, and to also cause them to fall silent instantly. It was in the castle of Mr. Tillemont whose ditches were so filled with crickets that one could hardly rest at night. We made some white wax in the sun with crocodile fat that is nearly as pure as whale oil; I even think that this whale oil would have the same effect as crocodile fat which is quite rare in this country. We formed a lamp of this composition with a fairly large candle, and it was not so soon lit and laid on the edge of the ditch, that the frogs stopped croaking.

The Hand of Glory

I confess that I never experienced the secret of the hand of glory; but I attended three times in the final judgment of some villains who confessed to having made and used them in crime. And as in the interrogation they were asked what it was, and how they had made it, and what was in use, they said, first, that the use of the hand of glory was to make those who are still alive, as those which are dead; secondly, that it was the hand of a hanged man; Third, that he must prepare it in the following manner. They take the hand of the man hanged by a road; it is wrapped in a piece of shroud, and it is pressed therein to release enough blood to make the shroud adhere to it; then it is put it in an earthen vessel with vinegar, saltpeter, salt, and black pepper, all ground up: it is left for fifteen days in the pot; then it is removed and exposed in the sunlight of the mid day until it dries completely. If the sun is not sufficient, they put it in an oven that is heated with fern and

THE PETIT ALBERT

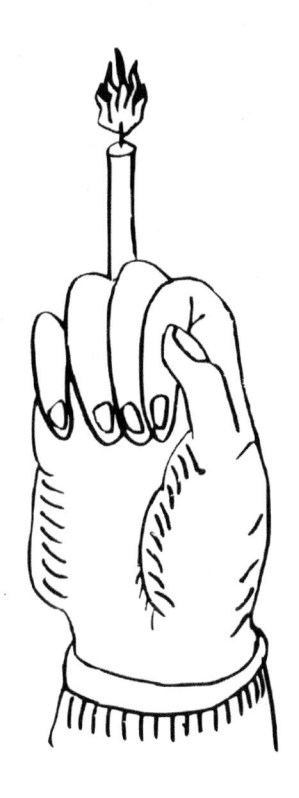

verbena.

A candle is then made with the fat of the hanged man, virgin wax, and sesame oil, and the hand of glory is then used as a candlestick to hold this candle when lit. In all the places where one shall go with this fatal instrument, all onlookers will become immobile. It was asked what remedy existed for such a device, and they said that the hand of glory became of no effect, and that thieves would

THE PETIT ALBERT

be defeated, if the threshold of the door of the house, or other places through which they attempt to enter with the hand, was smeared with an ointment composed of black cat blood, white chicken fat, and owl blood, upon a cloth there. It was necessary that this all was made during mid summer.

To Make a Person Insensible to Torture

To elaborate on the methods of criminals as before, I will report the details of what I learned of Mr. Bamberge, famous criminal judge at Oxfort. He said he had seen several times in certain cases there, that torture was sometimes insufficient to draw testimony from the charged, since their crimes had been committed in secret, and that it was difficult to find witnesses though there were strong presumptions against them, and that these people tried so hard to keep their crimes a secret that the court had to release others to secure their testimony. There are some as well who perform incantations to protect themselves from torture's effects. Others keep spells written on parchment, on their person. Here are three verses they speak when tortured, to defend against it.

Imparibus meritis tria during corporæ ramis.
Dismas et Gestas in medio is potestas divina.
Damnatur Dismas, Gestas have astra levatur.

Here are more words spoken when they are currently applied to torture.

As the pale and glorious Virgin Mary was sweet and gentle to our Lord Jesus Christ, such is this torture soft and the rope gentle to my body.

I recognized the first to use these kinds of charms, and he surprised us all by his resistance to torture; because after the first questioning, he seemed to sleep soundly as though in his own bed, without lamenting, complaining, or crying. When they had continued the torture a couple of times, he continued in his resistance which made us suspect that he was provided with some enchantment, and to check if this was the case, he was made to strip naked. After a thorough search, they found on him a small paper which was the figure of the three kings, with these words on the reverse: "Beautiful star, who delivered the magi from the persecution of Herod. Deliver me from this torment." This paper was stuffed into his left ear. However, although the court took this paper away, he did not let up even then, or at least he remained insensitive to torture, because when they applied it, he whispered under his breath, some words that could not be heard distinctly; And as he constantly persevered in denial. He had to be returned to prison until some stronger evidence against him was available. They say we can stop the effect of these mysterious words by uttering scriptural verses, or canonical material, like such: "My heart utters the truth; I will tell all my actions to the king, and he will declare my works. The Lord will open my lips, and my mouth shall proclaim truth. That sinner's wickedness is confused; you lose, Lord, all those who say lies."

An Ointment Which Protects Against Fire

There has been for several centuries the custom of

THE PETIT ALBERT

using fire to determine the guilt of criminals, but this custom was abolished because it is suspected that it is a way of tempting the Lord. Indeed, it has been discovered, from those times, from ancient historians, the length of time which the accused was suspended in the flames. And here is what I have gathered from the truth on this subject: To resist flame, make an ointment composed of hibiscus juice, fresh egg, mucous, sphylion seed, powdered lime, and horseradish juice. This is crushed and mixed all together, and rubbed on the whole body, if one will be tested as such, or just on the hands if the person is to be tortured just upon those. The ointment must be allowed to dry onto the body and can be applied as many as three times. This makes the user resistant to all fire.

Making Ardent Water

You will take a powerful aged wine, of strong color, and infuse into two pints of the same a pure chunk of limestone of a half pound of weight or about forty ounces of bright sulfur, with as much of good calcite and as much of common salt. This must all be ground up and pounded and mixed, then placed in a fluted vase. Distill this all on a slow fire up to three times to create your ardent water, which must be kept in a strong glass jar: Or else distill serpentine infused in wine and quicklime.

Making Greek Fire

This fire is so violent, it burns everything to which it is applied, but it can be extinguished by urine, vinegar, or sand. It is composed of powdered sulfur, tartar, resin, grain spirits, salt, and common oil. These things should be mixed well, such that a piece of cloth will burn instantly it sprayed with the same material. It should be mixed and removed using an iron mixer, and it should only be made outdoors, because should it immolate it will be extremely difficult to put out.

To Create Peace

I take leave of these violent materials, to say a few words about peace. I read in the book of curious secrets of King John of Aragon, that if someone, having observed that the Sun has entered the sign of Virgo, takes care to pluck a marigold, which was called by the ancients, Bride of the Sun, and if it is wrapped in bay leaves with a wolf's tooth, no one will speak evil of the man carrying the same, and he will live in profound peace and tranquility with all people.

On the Same Subject

We see in an old story in the History of France during the reign of Charles VII, that the prince, being in extreme consternation because of constant warfare, went to speak with to a holy hermit, which he desired prayer from. The holy man gave him an image of Veronica, with the following prayer which he had written on the reverse of the picture. He said that, if he was devout and recited the prayer daily, his business would recover from good to better. What happened shortly after was nothing short of a miracle, for the service that gave him the Maid of Orleans. And that is why many people carry this image now and recite the following prayer:

THE PETIT ALBERT

Pax Domini nostri Jesu Christi sic semper mecum per virtutem Heliæ Prophetae, cum potestate et efficacia faciei Domini nostri Salvatoris et dilectissimæ Matris ejus Sanctae Mariae Virginis, and per caput Sancti Joannis-Baptistae, and per duodecim Apostolos, and per foursome Evangelistas, and per sanctos omnes Martyrs Dei Confessores, Virgines, Viduas, Archangelos, Angelos & omnes denique celestial Hierarchias. Amen.

The Secret Garter For Travelers

You will collect a grass called mugwort, in the time that the Sun enters the first degree of Capricorn, and dry it in the shade. Make as well thin bands of flesh from a young hare, that is to say, having cut the hare's skin belts of the width of two inches, you will redouble the same, in which you sew the same mugwort. Wear these upon your legs, and there is no horse that will be able to keep pace with you. You can also apply the urine of a virgin to your legs at sunrise, and will not only relieve yourself of fatigue from any prior travel, but will travel further and more easily on the present day as well. Observe that at the time, the moon is in conjunction with Mercury. This observation will be even better, if done on a Wednesday of spring; then you will take a piece of cooked skin of a young wolf which you will make two garters on which you write with your blood the following words: Abumalith Cados ambulevit in Fortitudine cibi illius, and you'll be amazed how quickly you will walk, being provided with these garters on your legs. For fear that the writing could be erased, it will be good to cover the garters as well with white thread on the side of the same writing. There is also a way to make the garter which I read about in an old manuscript of Gothic letters: here is the recipe. You will take the hair of a hanged thief, which you shall braid, forming garters. You sew the same between two wires in such colors as you like: you will attach them to the hind legs of a young colt; thenforce the colt to walk backwards while invocating as follows: Sicut ambulat Dominus Sabaoth pennas Ventorum super, super sicut ambulabo terram. Let the colt escape and run until it tires. These garters are as effective as the others.

The Secret Stick For Travelers

You shall take the day after Halloween a strong branch of elderberry, to be used as a walking stick. Trim the tip off and cap it with an iron cap, and hollow the staff out, removing the core wood inside. Put at the bottom of the hollow stick both eyes of a young wolf, the tongue and heart of a dog, three green lizards, and three swallow hearts. All this to be dried in the sun between two sheets of paper, with the papers dusted with powdered saltpeter. Put above this material in the stick seven verbena leaves, picked the eve of St. John the Baptist, with a stone of various colors, found in the nest of a hoopoe bird, and close up the top of the staff with an whatever material you wish, and be assured that this staff will guarantee you protection from highwaymen, wild beasts, rabid dogs, and venomous snakes. It will also protect you at inns or places where you seek rest, guaranteeing the benevolence of the hosts.

The Secret to Making Horses Travel Quickly

THE PETIT ALBERT

Mix a handful of satyrion into the oats which you will feed your horse. Anoint the top of its four legs under the belly with deer fat. When you're ready to ride the horse, you will turn his head towards the rising sun and, into its left ear, you pronounce three times in a low voice, the following words, and your trip will be extremely fast: Caspar, Melchior, Merchisard. I add to this, if you suspend a necklace of wolf canines on the neck of the horse, the horse will not fear wolves.

To Make an Angry Horse Tame

There are small round stones of a green hue at the foot of Mount Cenis, which have the following ability; if you put one in each ear of a furious horse, and you clench his ears with each hand, the horse will become mild and be able to be ridden, and also not just easily ridden, but without any balking at all. The furious and untamed bull can become tame as well, if it is bound to a fig tree, and they make him take his food for some time under the tree. If elderberry bark is worn by the bull at the knee it will also cause it to become tame.

To Cause the Horse to Appear Deceased

You will take a snake tongue and wrap it into virgin wax, and lay it in the left ear of a horse; it will fall to the ground as if he was dead. As soon as you remove it it will stir again. Do not keep the horse in this condition for too long, lest it be injured or harmed.

THE PETIT ALBERT

The Ring of Invisibility

The famous Gyges of Lydia is reported, to have used a magical ring of invisibility to ascend to the throne of his land. It gave him the ease of committing adultery with the queen and allowed him to kill the king. The wise Kabbalists left us the method to manufacture such rings as have similar abilities. This operation must be begun on a Wednesday in spring under the auspices of Mercury, when one is sure that this planet will be in conjunction with other favorable planets, like the Moon, Jupiter, Venus or the Sun. Having good and purified mercury, you will form a large ring that can easily enter thefit onto the middle finger of the hand- place into the ring a little stone, of chrysoberyl, found in the nest of the hoopoe, and then brand the ring with the following words:

"Jesus passed through the midst of them"

Then, having placed the ring on a mercury plate, which will be made in the form of small palette, it will be scented with the perfume of Mercury, as has been spoken of in this same work previously. It must be treated with the same perfume thrive, and having wrapped the ring in a piece of cloth of suitable color for the planet, it should be deposited back in the same hoopoe nest where the chrysoberyl was first obtained- leave the ring there for nine days, and then remove it and once more scent it with its perfume. Then, keep it carefully in a small box made under the auspices of Mercury, to be used on occasions where the ring is needed.

The way to use it is none other than to wear the ring

with the stone facing outwards as any other ring. It has the virtue of dazzling bystanders such that they do not pay attention to the wearer. And when one wishes again to be seen, turn the stone to face the inside of the hand, making a fist around it. Porphyry, Iamblichus, Peter de Abano, and Agrippa, all speak of a similar ring, as in the figure shown here, which they say has the same virtue and property. You have to take hairs from the forehead of a hyena, and make a ring by braiding the same- and it is similarly stored in a hoopoe nest for nine days and scented with perfume, all as before. The only difference here is that, to regain visibility, one must remove the ring from the finger entirely.

To See Fascinating Things With the Ring

As there is no poison in nature without its antidote, the wise providence of the Creator who made everything with weight and measures did not allow any disease for which no cure is possible. If we want therefore to take precautions against the effect of the ring of Mercury, there will be another ring composed in the following manner. Form a ring with refined lead purified as remarked on previously in this work, accounting for the cycles of the celestial region. In the ring must be placed the eye of a weasel, and on the ring's edge, the following is engraved: "Apparuit Dominus Simoni". The ring must be formed on a Saturday, when Saturn will be in opposition to Mercury: three times will the perfume of Saturday be used upon it, and then wrap it in burial cloth, depositing it for nine days in the cemetery before taking it again to use.

Those who invented this ring, based this all on the

concept of opposites, which lies between the materials that make up these two rings that have such opposite effects. Indeed, there is nothing more repugnant to the hyena than the weasel. And Saturn is almost always retrograde to Mercury; or when they meet in the home of some of the signs of the zodiac, it is always a bad reaction and quite ominous.

To Manufacture Other Rings Under the Auspices of the Planets

It was assumed heretofore that each planet has its metal appropriate to its heavenly constitution. To now proceed with the creation of such rings as we spoke of, we will say that it is not only necessary to use the metals which coincide with the planets, but also the stones which relate to their constitutions and the engravings which shall encircle their mysterious figure. The Aetite and Zircon are solar in nature, the Emerald is lunar, Amethyst is under Mars. The Topaz and Porphyry are suitable for Mercury; Beryl is specific to the Jupiter; Carnelian be for Venus and Jasper for Saturn. Care should always be taken to craft such rings in times suitable for their respective constellations using their proper stones, and to properly form the mysterious figures to be engraved on said stones which we have given the models heretofore to be engraved upon the stones themselves in where we spoke of talismans. It is not so easy to burn the figures on the stones as opposed to upon metals where you can print with irons; it is good to warn those who undertake these operations, that they should begin their work at the first moment of the favorable time for the planet, and they must continue without abandon, and when complete, the ring will have the desired value and influence. Here is a model for hours, as for the day so for the night, which will allow this work with ease.

The Hours of the Day and Night

We should always begin with the daylight hours of Sunday. At the first dominates the Sun, the second Venus, the third Mercury, the fourth the Moon, the fifth Saturn, the sixth Jupiter, at the seventh Mars, at the eighth the Sun, at the ninth Venus, at the tenth Mercury, at the eleventh the Moon, at the twelth Saturn.

Sunday, the hours of the night.

The first in Jupiter, the second in March, the third in the Sun, the fourth in Venus, the fifth in Mercury, the sixth in the Moon, the seventh in Saturn, the eighth in Jupiter, the ninth in Mars, the tenth in the Sun, the eleventh in Venus, the twelfth in Mercury.

Monday, the hours of the day.

The first in the Moon, the second in Saturn, the third in Jupiter, the fourth in Mars, the fifth in the Sun, the sixth in Venus, the seventh in Mercury, the eighth in the Moon, the ninth in Saturn, the tenth in Jupiter, the eleventh in Mars, the twelfth in the Sun.

Monday, the hours of the night.

The first in Venus, the second in Mercury, the third

THE PETIT ALBERT

in the Moon, the fourth in Saturn, the fifth in Jupiter, the sixth in Mars, the seventh in the Sun, the eighth in Venus, the ninth in Mercury, the tenth in the Moon, the eleventh in Saturn, The twelfth in Jupiter.

On Tuesday, the hours of the day.

The first in Mars, the second in the Sun, the third in Venus, the fourth in Venus, the fifth in the Moon, the sixth in Saturn, the seventh in Jupiter, the eighth in Mars, the ninth in the Sun, the tenth in Venus, the eleventh in Mercury, The twelfth in the Moon.

Tuesday, the hours of the night.

The first in Saturn, the second in Jupiter, the third in Mars, the fourth in the Sun, The fifth in Venus, the sixth in Mercury, the seventh in the Moon, the eighth in Saturn, the ninth in Jupiter, the tenth in Mars, the eleventh in the Sun, the twelfth in Venus.

Wednesday, the hours of the day.

The first in Mercury, the second in the Moon, the third in Saturn, the fourth in Jupiter, the fifth in Mars, the sixth in the Sun, the seventh in Venus, the eighth in Mercury, the ninth in the Moon, the tenth in Saturn, the eleventh in Jupiter, the twelfth in Mars.

Wednesday, the hours of the night.

The first in the Sun, the second in Venus, the third

THE PETIT ALBERT

in Mercury, the fourth in the Moon, the fifth in Saturn, the sixth in Jupiter, the seventh in Mars, the eighth in the Sun, the ninth in Venus, the tenth in Mercury, the eleventh in the Moon, the twelfth in Saturn.

Thursday, the hours of the day.

The first in Jupiter, the second in Mars, the third in the Sun, the fourth in Venus, the fifth in Mercury, the sixth in the Moon, the seventh in Saturn, the eighth in Jupiter, the ninth in Mars, the tenth in the Sun, the eleventh in Venus, the twelfth in Mercury.

Thursday, the hours of the night.

The first in the Moon, the second in Saturn, the third in Jupiter, the fourth in Mars, the fifth in the Sun, the sixth in Venus, the seventh in Mercury, the eighth in the Moon, the ninth in Saturn, the tenth in Jupiter, the eleventh in Mars, the twelfth in the sun.

Friday, the hours of the day.

The first in Venus, the second in Mercury, the third in the Moon, the fourth in Saturn, the fifth in Jupiter, the sixth in Mars, the seventh in the Sun, the eighth in Venus, the ninth in Mercury, the tenth in the Moon, the eleventh in Saturn, the twelfth in Jupiter.

Friday, the hours of the night.

The first in Mars, the second in the Sun, the third in

THE PETIT ALBERT

Venus, the fourth in Mercury, the fifth in the Moon, the sixth in Saturn, the seventh in Jupiter, the eighth in Mars, the ninth in the Sun, the tenth in Venus, the eleventh in Mercury, the twelfth in the Moon.

Saturday, the hours of the day.

The first in Saturn, the second in Jupiter, the third in Mars, the fourth in the Sun, the fifth in Venus, the sixth in Mercury, the seventh in the Moon, the eighth in Saturn, the ninth in Jupiter, the tenth in Mars, the eleventh in the Sun, the twelfth in Venus.

Saturday, the hours of the night.

The first in Mercury, the second in the Moon, the third in Saturn, the fourth in Jupiter, the fifth in Mars, the Sixth in the Sun, the seventh in Venus, the eighth in Mercury, the ninth in the Moon, the tenth in Saturn, the eleventh in Jupiter, the twelfth in Mars.

Observations of the planets as such in their hours are not the least important of things which must be regarded by occultists: it shows that the figures of the planets are each located at the first hour of his day, without anticipating one over the other, or interrupting their order in all the hours of the day of the week, and it was observed that it is generally at those times that the planets have favorable aspects; and those who want to work with mysterious figures upon talismans, will do so upon this continuing order, and the arrangement of hours thereby, because one would not craft one figure in the period in which another is to be made.

The Philosophers Regarding Talismans

The sages who have applied themselves to discover the origins of the names that were given to things, and above all those that contain something extraordinary, say that the word "talisman" comes from Hebrew and means "image." Some have said that this word is from "telesma", the Greek word, which means perfection; others say that it originates from these two Latin words, "talis mens." When one is expert in the Kabbalistic sciences, one can make talismans according to his thought, to his intentions, and his wishes as they are: the former is awarded by these two Latin words. But anyways regardless it is known that these arts originate in Egypt and also from the Chaldaeans, who were above all else so learned in astronomy, and had penetrated in all the virtues and efficiencies of their influences, and in fact had a practical science whose use began to gain the highest of note. The Hebrews who came to Egypt when Joseph governed under the reign of the Pharaoh learned from them these mysteries. They perfected these arts by speaking with the Chaldaeans who made their heavenly figures to attract the influences of the stars, because they sharply observed their progress, the diversity of their aspects and conjunctions, to draw their predictions which served to regulate their life and their fortune.

Balm Oil Extracted From Heavenly Water

If balm oil is placed in the ears three drops at a time only a few times a day and cotton applied, it may heal deafness. It can also heal any kind of gall or ringworm, even the most inveterate kind. It may also treat all wounds, scars, or ulcers. It treats the bites of venomous snakes or spiders, along with all fistulas, cramps, and corpuscles. It may be applied as a plaster as well to treat the limbs and can silence heart palpitations. Crollius actually so much esteems it, that he called it "mother balm oil," claiming it to be superior to all others.

Balm to Prevent Plague

This recipe can destroy any plague, it was a gift of a King of Spain to his daughter, Queen of France, designed by his own physician. It is simple enough so that anyone may concoct it. You must obtain twelve black salsify roots, and cook them in three quarts of white wine, and make sure that the pot where they cook is well covered for fear of too much evaporation of the alcohol; then being cooked you place them in a cloth and press the roots to extract the juices soaked into them. Add to this liquor juice twelve lemons, a half ounce of ginger, half an ounce of cloves, a half ounce of cardamom, half an ounce of aloe wood, all well crushed.

To this mixture you must join one ounce or so of the following; elderberry, brambles, and frank sage. You will boil it all together and quite slowly until decreasing the liquid to one quart, and then very quickly the material must be cooled. Then put it in a glass jar strong and sealed tightly. Drink the potion on an empty stomach every morning for nine days and by this means you will be the test of the miasmas, when Even you are among plague victims. For those who are already infected, add to the drink the juice of a bugloss root and dried scabiosa, and this will be an antidote to the contagion within them. For plague wounds, mix pileront leaves, brambles, elderberries, mustard seed, and coal dust, and make this into a poultice to apply to the wounds. By God's help they will heal.

To Remove Rotten Teeth Painlessly

Infuse mulberry roots in vinegar. After having done so, you add to it a good spoon of Roman vitriol, and will expose this mix it in the summer sun for fifteen days in a strong glass jar; then dry them all in a glazed earthenware pot, with a green lizard, in a moderately hot oven, the pot being well covered. You will make this all into a powder, which you will put on the decayed tooth, and it will fall out on its own in a short time.

To Cure Gunshots or Other Wounds

You will make a decoction as listed thus. Taking two crown's weight of dutchman's pipe, some laurel seed, and crayfish dried in a smith's oven and harvested on a full moon, also powdered musk, of one shield's weight, and four crown's weight of comfrey or brunelle grass. It is necessary this final herb is harvested with its flowers, and dried in the shade between two cloths. You will reduce all these to fine powder, and after having mixed well, you will put them in a sachel of new cloth, which is closed with a wire; then you will have an earthen pot, glazed, in which you put your bag, with twenty small branches of periwinkle and three pints of the best white wine you can find, and after having plugged your pot with three or four sheets of paper, such that steam can be released only from a small area, you will put it into a charcoal fire, and it will boil and be reduced to a third of its original volume. When you remove it from the fire, and having allowed it to cool, you must place this decoction in a double fine linen, and lay it in a strong glass jar to serve you in need; beware above all that the jar is closed such that air does not enter it.

Here is how it is used for healing wounds. You will have a small syringe made of copper, which is always kept clean, so that it may be used on wounds that are hollow as follows. You gently clean the wound with a small white cloth, soaked in the decoction as listed, and then you use the syringe to inject the decoction into the wound three or four times, and you will cover the wound with the cloth and with the leaf of a red cabbage to seal it and put more of the decoction into the leaves forming a compress. Wrap the wound lightly, and it will heal shortly. Beware to keep it clean as the wound closes, as to not let the wolf into the sheep's pen, so to speak.

On the Same Subject

I witnessed with astonishment the prompt manner in which a Polish soldier healed one of his comrades which had been stabbed twice, without any medicine at all, for the wounds should have been fatal. He began by washing his mouth with alcohol, then with rose water, so having fresh breath and without bad smell; then approaching the sick. He saw the wound that was all bloody, and having cleaned the same by washing with water in which plantain had been boiled, it quenched all the blood flow, and he pressed a cloth soaked in the same plantain washings into the wound. He then uttered the following words, making the sign of the cross on the wound with each statement, as marked here: "Jesus Christ was born, Jesus Christ died, Jesus Christ was resurrected, Jesus Christ commands the blood of the wound to stop flowing, Jesus Christ commands the wound to close, Jesus Christ commands the wound not to fester, as the five wounds on his holy body." then he went on to say: "Sword, I command thee in the name and by the power of the one to whom all creatures bow, do not do more harm to that creature, than the lance that pierced the sacredness of Jesus Christ, who is hanging from the tree of the cross: In the name of the Father and of the Son and of the holy Spirit, Amen."

If anyone should suffer such a stabbing wound such that the wound goes entirely through them, one must make the same ceremony for the other side, and it is covered with a compress soaked in the same plantain water, this being done every twelve hours. The patient will recover quickly.

To Treat Sprains of the Feet

We must undertake this healing quickly when needed and not wait if possible, and the sprained foot will be healed swiftly. Whoever makes the operation should take his left shoe and use it to touch three times the bad foot, forming sign of the cross with the same left foot pronouncing these words. For the first time, say "ante" and make the sign of the cross. The second time you say and do the same. For the third time, say "super ante you" and make the sign of the cross. The patient must be touched on the sprain each time. This can also treat horses, not just men.

Those who advise others that these are merely superstitions should know that more skilled people than they have given their approval of medical secrets that are just as strange and whose causes are just as mysterious. Who is it, for example, which can explain by proper and normal methods, what I read in a book of secrets, printed in Paris, with approval and privilege, an infallible remedy for curing insomnia or excessive sleepiness, which is to take a big toad, and at once separate the head from the body, and then to dry the head? And each time this is done, when the

THE PETIT ALBERT

head is separated, one eye is always open and the other always closed, and that a person who needs sleep must be concerned with the closed eye while the person who wishes to resist sleep makes use of the open one? Moreover, what of powdered human skull, with the wonderful property of healing ulcers so quickly? It even seems contrary to reason, and to the principles of medicine, when we say that opposites are cured by opposites. However, this author, approved and privileged, denotes that the skull powder, which is only corruption, heals other corruptions, and on the strength of this author, a president of Paris, that is to say a man of good spirit and sound judgment, is the test of these secrets with great success without fear of being superstitious.

This same author, approved and privileged, said that to break the lanyard curse aforementioned, it is necessary that the person wears a small bag hanging from her neck with three kinds of materials: coccifera, artemesia absinthium, and mistletoe. Coccifera picked September 23, artemisia and the mistletoe, picked June 24, before sunrise. The same author has spoken of other issues, as such:

To cast off the evil eye one must burn a dead snake upon coals and allow the smoke to rise into the face.

There is also an approach to treating blindness, which is to mix mud and spittle and anoint the eyes of the blind as spoken of in the Bible.

The seed or seeds of nettle, can prevent boils, if they are simply cooked in with your dinner in a pot,

THE PETIT ALBERT

allowing the steam or smoke to surround you.

To prevent bad encounters in travel, it is necessary, says this author, to put the tongue of a snake in the sheath of your sword.

To prevent a musket from shooting sideways and missing, you have to rub onion juice upon the end of the muzzle.

There are in this book endorsed a large number of other secrets, which are not authorized by reason, yet it remains wise in not constantly advancing to the point of superstition relating to the occult or unknown causes. As Pliny says, as to prevent scorpions from entering homes, particularly in countries where these insects and others are common, it is necessary that we take care to hang above the door, inside the house, a small bag in which there are hazelnuts; this is explained by the antipathy between such creatures and hazel- hazelnut which is the fruit; horseradish similarly in itself a great antipathy with scorpions, and by applying it to them, it will destroy the scorpion.

The same Pliny says that to prevent the vines from being damaged by hail or frosts, two young men must take a rooster, and stationing themselves near the vineyards, they entwine the rooster by a leg and a wing using ropes, and will then tug on the rooster such that it rips it apart; then they will tour the vineyards turning their backs to each other; and spraying the rooster blood around the vineyard at intervals. Where they meet circling around in the rows, they bury the parts of the torn rooster. This prevents hail, storms, and animals from damaging the vineyard. Some others claim that by burning or roasting a lizard liver on a coal fire in a field or vineyard, this perfume can dissipate a storm.

I have been told by some villagers as well, that they had repeatedly conjured away hail storms, by merely presenting a mirror opposite of the clouds. Similarly, by linking together several keys of various houses with a small rope, and storing these keys on the ground in a circle.

Put a turtle on its shell, such that it can't get up or walk, it is very certain that as long as it is in this posture, hail or storm does fall point in the or in the field vinefield or vineyard. These are things done daily by such villagers which they learned from their ancestors from father to son.

Of Mandrakes

Although most villagers live in ignorance and stupidity of a coarse kind, nevertheless they have some acquaintance with and practice of occultism which is most admirable. I remember staying with a rich farmer, who had once been very poor and miserable, so he was forced to work constantly. As I had known him in the time of his misery, I took occasion to ask him what he had done to become rich in a short time. He told me that a gypsy had been stealing his chickens, and he had beaten the gypsy, and she had then taught him the secret of the mandrake, and that since that time he had always thrived from good to better, and hardly a day went by that he didn't attain some more wealth. Here is in what way the Bohemian had taught him to use the mandrake which I show the figure of here.

One must take a bryonia root, which is shaped roughly in a human figure; it is taken out of the ground in the spring on a Monday, when the Moon is in a happy constellation, or in conjunction with Jupiter in amicable appearance with Venus. Cut the ends of the root, as gardeners do when they want to transplant a plant, then it must be buried in a cemetery in the middle of the grave of a dead man, and water it before sunrise for a month, with cow whey, in which there will be three drowned bats. It is then removed and will be in an even more human-like form. It is dried in an oven fired with verbena wood, and it must be stored in burial cloth. As long as one is in possession of the mysterious root, it will increase luck greatly, especially at gambling. That's how the peasant told me he had become wealthy.

There are also mandrakes of another kind, and these are claimed to be leprechauns, goblins, or familiar spirits, and which serve several purposes; some are visible in the shape of animals, and others are invisible. I found myself in a castle where there had been a man which for six years maintained the clock and grounds there and cared for the horses. He told me of two things with all the accuracy that one could wish, and I was curious to see him the next morning. My astonishment was great when I saw him driving horses withouteven touching them. The groomer told me he had attracted to his service a leprechaun, by taking a little black hen, and bleeding it at a cross road; And that the blood of the chicken, he had taken, and used to write on a small piece of paper: "Berit will do my work for

THE PETIT ALBERT

twenty years, and I will reward him," and having buried the chicken under the road a foot down, the same day the leprechaun had taken care of the clock and horses, and that from time to time, he made finds that were worth something.

Some people stubbornly believe in these beings, which they call mandrakes, and they pay them a tribute daily, of a small sum. I do not say this except to illustrate their practice. And all those who have spoken to me about the same generally did not tell me anything except that when one attracts these kinds of mandrakes to his service, they are happy to help and will allow the finding of money or jewels by road sides, and that they can use dreams to inspire one with such service to find treasure.

I will end this matter by the story of a mandrake I saw in Metz in the hands of a wealthy Jew, he was a little monster roughly similar to figure I give here engraved; it was no bigger than a fist; this little monster had lived only five weeks, and in such a short time had made the fortune of this Jew, who confessed that he was, on the the seventh day, inspired while sleeping to go in an old hut, where he found a very considerable amount of coined money, and a lot of silver as well, and that since then he had always thrived in business. He surprised me well, telling me how he had had this mandrake. I followed, and he told me, that the famous Avicenna wrote about this, that you need a large egg of black hen, which you pierce, draining some of the insides, about the size of a bean, and then put human seed into the egg, plugging the hole with a bit of moist parchment. It will be incubated beginning on the first day of the Moon in Mars in a happy constellation of Mercury and Jupiter. After the proper time, the egg will hatch, and out comes a little monster as you see. Worms and asps must be fed to it; the one you see only lived space of one month and five days. And after it died it was pickled in a jar of good wine to preserve it and its effects.

Explanations of the Heavenly Talismans

The two talismans that you see etched below from mandrake were taken from the Clavicle of Solomon, the original is in in the cabinet of the Duke of Lithuania: they were made by the scientist Rabin-Isaac Radiel, both under the auspices of the planet Mercury, as it is easy to judge from the characters that are marked on the second. Their powers involve trading, travel and games of chance, their composition is one that suits Mercury. Those who want to learn the nature of this Kabbalistic science of talismans, can read diligently the works of Paracelsus, of Cardau, of Jamblic, Porta, of Gaffarel, Helmont, Hermes Trismegistus, Agrippa, Coclenius, Monecjus, and Fludd. All of these authors discuss these matters with astrological principles, within Kabbala and the natural sciences.

A Healing Powder

All those who have used this wonderful secret, until now, have endeavored by great physical arguments to prove the reality of the same. As it is difficult to speak clearly about something that is in itself extremely obscure and hidden, it is no wonder that these physicists have not converted many unbelievers nor convinced academics by

THE PETIT ALBERT

reasoning; Digby Knight attempts to explain the powers he speaks of but yet the masses neither believe nor understand these works, for he presumes these secrets to be real, while we all seek the reason behind the secret and evidence for the same. He also presumes the principles behind the same secrets.

You have to have good Roman vitriol that is calcined, or rather which is purified of its superfluous humidity, exposing it for three or four days in the hot sun, being enclosed in a glass vial well corked. The Vitriol must be diluted in a small bowl of rainwater, filtered into the fire, about one ounce to a pint of water. If this is to be done in summer, one does not bring the water close to the fire, because it is necessary that it is neither cold nor hot, but in a just temperament between the cold and the hot; then this concoction has a linen dipped into it and some of the patient's blood is dipped into the same with the linen.

If the patient is away from the place that the operation is taking place, it could not be more convenient for evidence of the healing and supernatural power we speak of; it suffices to dip the same linen at noon into the vitriolic water, and to hold this bowl in a cool place. Every time the linen is mixed with the blood, the patient will feel their pain relieved to the degree of the work of a skillful surgeon. The patient will be cured in a very short time, by the invaluable virtue of vitriol, which we shall have occasion to speak of also elsewhere.

THE PETIT ALBERT

Making Gold Artificially

It's not just by digging and searching in the bowels of the earth that gold is obtained. Art can imitate nature on this point, since nature perfects in many other things. I will say here what has been proven countless times, and which has become very common among those who work in the great work of alchemy. You will need a crucible fit for extreme heat, having put on a good burning stove, you must apply rosin powder to the bottom of the crucible, the thickness of a finger, and you spread upon this rosin a thin layer of iron filings, applying a thin dusting of red sulfur upon the same. Melt the iron using a great fire, operating the bellows, then throw borax upon it, melting this all down; you will throw the same quantity of red arsenic in, and as much copper as you used iron filings, and let this all cook, working the fire to great intensity, careful not to breathe the fumes because of the arsenic. You will have another crucible in which you will add the annealed material by measures, having previously mixed the heated materials well with an iron spatula, and you will ensure that it flows into this second crucible, purified and without waste; by means of the water separator, through which the gold will fall to the bottom of the vessel. When you have collected the gold, you'll melt it in a crucible, and you will have beautiful gold that will compensate you for your trouble and expense. I took this secret from a book with the title, "The Sealed Cabinet." The ease with which it can succeed invited me to do the experiment several times, each time more easily, and as suchI found it consistent in its execution. Thus says very learned Basil Valentine, that the trial of the great work of philosophers can be done in less than three or four days, that the expenditure does not exceed the sum of three or four florins, and that three or four earthen vessels may suffice.

Another Method

Here is another way left to us by Caravana, of the Spanish American colonies. You will take strong sulfur, nitrate salt, saltpeter, each in the same amount, that is to say, about four ounces each; all being well pulverized. Put the same into a large glass vessel, well luted, and filled with loam; this must be put to a low flame, for the space of two hours, then increased in heat until it makes no smoke, the smoke released after a flame out of the neck of the vessel by the small holes there. This flame being discontinued, we will see sulfur precipitate in the vessel, fixed and of a white color. This must be taken, adding sal ammoniac and pilera to it, pulverizing it all together gently, and it will sublimate starting with a slow fire, and will gradually grow in volume until it rises within four hours. Remove the contents of the vessel, as well as whatever has caked onto the bottom; you will incorporate this all and sublime it all together again, continuing this way of sublimation up to six times; after which the sulfur is at the bottom of the vessel, which will be collected and pounded on a wet slab of stone, and this same material will turn into an oil. Six drops of golden ducat must be placed in the crucible, and the oil placed on a marble to freeze. Fifty measures of mercury can be transformed into gold with this oil, heated with the same crucible.

THE PETIT ALBERT

Another Method, From England

As well might it be that the real operators of the great philosophical art are unanimously agreed that the Moon, that is to say, spirit, is in itself, and as to its substance, the real Sun, that is, gold, the same, and these twain make perfection when mixed. For reaching that perfect concoction, we shall proceed in this way, to test the secret, you will prepare an ash composed of wood branch, and cow bones, burned until they appear white as snow; you must grind this ash, and lay it in a glazed earthen vessel that you fill with forge water, and add as much quicklime as there is ash. Boil it all together until the water is diminished by half, and then set for four ounces of good fine silver, which you have beaten into small blades, about the thickness of a nail; you will make your silver into twelve of these blades and throw them in the pot with your ashes in decoction, and continue to boil until the water is reduced by half of what formerly remained. Then you remove your twelve silver blades, cleaning them with a white cloth, and leave them to rest. The composition present in the vase will be formed on the surface of the sides, comprised of a salt in the form of crystal, it will need to be collected by a tin instrument.

You will pour some more forge water in the vase, and will boil it again and then cool it to remove the salt that forms on the surface. Continue these boilings, until your composition renders almost no salt; add to this philosophical salt fourfold another salt called vegetable salt, which is composed of sulfur, saltpeter, and tartar, in the manner that good artists and apothecaries know.

THE PETIT ALBERT

Besides that, you will take four times as much of good red clay which you can obtain in tile form; you will reduce this to a fine powder, and will make thin golden blades, as you did silver, making sure the total weight of the gold is the same as that of the silver you formerly utilized. Use the best crucible available, and additionally you will make a bed of powder comprised of your salt, your cement, red earth, and a little borax which is used by goldsmiths. For the first layer, you will put a thin golden plate, covering this with a second layer of your salts and earth, then place a second golden plate thereupon, and do so until the twelfth, which will be similarly covered like the others, then you will put this in your luted vessel within the crucible and set it to the fire, and be assured that in this manner it will melt properly.

This being completed, you will have another vessel in which there is an opening that can be opened and closed when you like. Once upon the crucible, add a blade of gold with some borax, and when you have reason to believe that gold is melted, you'll open the vessel and add one of your silver blades to the same, so that the gold devours it and is nourished. You will continue, and each day, throw a silver blade in the vessel until they are all devoured by the gold, taking great care to keep the fire in the same balance, so that the matter can always be melted. When your last blade of silver is added, you can leave off your fire and cool the vessel, in which you will find almost double the gold as you had put it. This will be a very good method by which to increase gold, following exactly the method I have just given. This method can be multiplied to any degree.

THE PETIT ALBERT

Another Method

If the great name of Aristeas was not famous among artists of the great work, we would have hardly believe what he says in this writing; he addresses his students by his statement in the manner of the great philosophical work; we discover through the obscurities of this writing, that Aristeas had thought that the mysterious stone of philosophers should be created from compressed air, rendered tangible: here is how he instructed his students on this great subject.

My students, having given you the knowledge of all things, and having taught you how you ought to live, and how you adjust your behavior thus by the maxims of excellent philosophy; after you learned also what concerns the order and the nature of the monarchy of the universe, I am left with another thing to communicate to you regarding the keys of nature, I have so far preserved this secret with very great care. Before all these other keys, one first must take place that is closed to the sublime nature of science: it is the general source of all things, and we do not doubt that God has given this any particular divine property.

When in possession of this key, riches become miserable, especially as there is no treasure that can be compared to him. Indeed, of what use are riches, when one is about to be afflicted by human infirmities? What good are the treasures, when one is felled by death? There is no wealth that we should not abandon when death takes hold of us. It is not the same when I possess this key.

THE PETIT ALBERT

I do not know if I have to say something here on the basis of an Arab who wrote about these kinds of materials. This ensures that these elixirs being joined together, with such gravity, creates the finest gold of life, or, gold precipitate, invariably crafted with the stone of the philosophers; he claims that this operation must be in a stronger glass vial of fired sand, and that the calcination which remains at the bottom of the vial can multiply up to one hundred thousand parts, and it is foolproof.

To Precipitate Gold

Take two ounces of quicksilver, cleaned and mixed with salt and vinegar, attach it to a powdered bit of gold the weight of a drachma, and knead well these two materials together in a glazed earthen dish that is kept slightly warmed so that they are well mixed: this mixing is called, commonly, making an amalgam. Pour this mix into cold water; if the quicksilver remains somewhat unmixed, then you need to use a leather bag to purify the substance and to join your amalgam, then wash with salt and vinegar distilled until no material remains of itself; the quicksilver will be reduced by this method of purification and mixing, such that for a golden drachma's weight of gold which you began with, there will be eight fine silver drachmas. Then you put the amalgam in a strong glass vessel that is still well luted and well clogged with loam, and pour over two ounces of etching, and then fire the composition, placing the material in bit by bit: it may require up to five additions in this manner, after which you will find at the bottom of the alembic a powder which you must put in an earthen vessel which will be fired at greater heat; you should water this powder with good rose water, and having the vessel so clogged that nothing can evaporate, you will put it to the stove and cook it until the fire is bright red, and the precipitated gold shall be complete.

It has the ability to cure the plague of syphilis, leprosy, dropsy, and other diseases which are so difficult to cure: it can cure intestinal blockage, liver obstructions, and it is beneficial to those who drank poison or which ate spoiled meat; it is used for curing bad ulcers and boils, either by taking it in some liquor or mixing with ointment into a plaster; all it takes is to give the weight of half a penny diluted in two tablespoons of syrup good for women and young people, and the weight of a penny diluted in a half glass of good wine for the old.

To Dissolve Gold

I learned of a monk, who was a great chemist, of such great ability that the Queen of France was astonished and would listen to nobody else on any subject he spoke of if the monk gave his approval by Jesus. The monk learned that the blood of a deer is a quick dissolver of gold. Here is the recipe: you take two bottles filled with the blood of a freshly killed deer, distilling it by heating it in a water bath up to five times, always distilling repeatedly whatever remains upon each of the five successive evaporations, then store what remains in a strong glass vial. This material is so good and so easily used for the dissolving of gold, that you can test the same on your hand without being harmed.

THE PETIT ALBERT

Another Method

Take two ounces of saltpeter, half an ounce of sulfur, half an ounce of crushed walnut shell dried well; you will reduce all this to fine powder together, making sure to fully crush all the walnut shell fragments. Place a small blade of gold on top of a layer of this powder in a bowl, which should be the width of a finger, and cover it also with another layer so that it is fully coated all around. You will see from experience that the blade will melt to the bottom of the bowl, without the material being heated at all: the experiment is done the same way for the other metals.

Turning Lead Into Gold

There are many people who reject as uncertain the method that the great chemist Fallopius employed to turn lead into pure gold, because it seems too easy for a work of this importance, yet it is not only Falopius who speaks of this in this way, for Basile Valentin and Odomarus say about the subject almost the same thing as Fallopius. Anyway, here is in what way he says it can be done: You will brew a bundle of Cyclamen with a bucket of forge water, making it clear through filtration; the infusion should be twenty four hours, so that the color is fully incorporated and liquefied into the water; then you distill this filtrate with pieces of felt fabric, and after this, filter it through sand as well, and you will keep this distillation in a strong glass jar, tightly capped, and then you put an ounce of good purified bright silver in the crucible, covering it to prevent evaporation. When you can assume that it has begun to boil, add an ounce of gold foil, pounded very thin, and withdraw the crucible from the flame. This being done, take a lead book endpure lead ingot and melt it, then incorporate the gold composition and quicksilver you have prepared well, mixing those three things together on the fire with an iron pole. When everything is well mixed, add an ounce of your filtrate water, and let digest it all together on your fire for a short space of time, and when the composition is cooled, you will find that it will be good gold. Note that lead is prepared and purified in this way. To have a purified ingot, vinegar, four ounces' worth, must be poured over the ingot to remove slag and evaporate it, then having melted the ingot for the first time, it is soaked in strong vinegar, is cleaned, and then also placed in celadine juice. It is melted again and cooled in salt water. Finally it is melted one last time and cooled in vinegar again, in which there will be evaporated quicklime, and it will be well purified.

To Create Fake Money Using Tin

The two ingots must be respectively of tin as is mined in Cornwall, and of refined lead, each a pound and a half in weight, as I explained heretofore. You put your tin in a vessel able to resist high flame and heat; the tin must be chopped into tiny pieces, and it will be joined to four ounces of quicksilver in the time it will start to boil in the vessel, and a moment after you remove it from the fire, and you put the lead ingot in the vessel, similarly chopped apart; then you adjust the retort so that you can, without fear of a sudden evaporation of quicksilver, boil the fire to depletion until you see that the quicksilver begin to bubble and splatter from the neck of the vessel's drip opening, and it will then utterly consumed. You will find at the bottom of the retort your tin transmuted, then blend it up to three times with a good ounce of flaxseed oil each time; then the last time and, at the final time, you'll need to spend a good while melting the same in boiling lye and gravel, and you'll find it at the bottom of the vessel; you still will melt it one more time with the oil, and then form the same into an ingot or in such other form as you please after making sure the material is now homogenized. After all these repeated works, three and a quarter pounds of matter that you had in the beginning will remain at least two and a half pounds in weight, of a metal that can pass for real money, firm and metallic.

Using Borax To Melt Gold

Whereas borax is a drug extremely necessary for operations involving gold and silver, I think it will not be out of place to give here the way to use it to create great value to spare the expense. The ancients were confounded by borax of chrysocolle, which they had in natural and artificial form, whose property is to promptlyset on fire a metal body and bring together in one body the divided parts of gold and silver; in short, it serves any work where one needs a prompt and sudden infusion. Borax both real and artificial. It usually comes from Alexandria if it relates to the writings of the ancient chemists, and they always came to that country, and it is thus that takes its name from the Alexandrian niter. Yet it is probable that it was brought from the Indies to Alexandria as well: I have seen a relationship that explains it this way the manner in which

THE PETIT ALBERT

the Indians wear the same stone, and preserve it amd put it in condition to be transported wherever they wish. We find the same in the mining of gold and silver- it is collected with the mud on which it is found; they put it to boil for some time and is then poured through cheesecloth or a cloth, and allowed to cool, and it forms small stones as niter does, and experience has made known that by keeping these stones for a long time, they crumble into mere dust; so to prevent that from happening, they are preserved, so to speak, and they are encased in fat mixed with the same mire from which they were formed, from mud. This mud is kneaded with fat, and is made into a paste; then having been ground up in a bowl, commensurate with the amount that is needed, a first layer is made of this paste, and it is covered with these stones; then a second layer of said paste similarly covers of these stones, and thus consecutively this is performed until the container is full of the stones encased in this mix, and finally one final layer is added such that the stones are completely encased, and it is all covered with wooden layers with earth on top, and is left like this for some months. When the material is to be transported it is done in this manner, and this is why the stones are smooth and shiny, with their fat. Women who know how to distill this paste use it as makeup, for which it is excellent.

Here is what can be done with this artificial borax, which has the same property as natural borax, some of the same being even better than the natural. The batter, so long as it isn't molding, is used, and ten pounds of it are placed in twelve pints of boiling water with two pounds of olive oil: one will need to skim this mix off, and we it is allowed to boil until everything is cooked, and it must be reduced in liquidity, such that if one puts a bit on a polished piece of wood, it will remain as a thick syrup in consistency; for when we take it away from the fire, and this is poured through a clear mixer, a small amount of the material is set aside for use later in this process, an amount about the same as would close the opening of the vessel it is filtered in. The mix is encased in horse manure for ten days then, removing any crust that forms upon it if needed, and then the rest of the material will be like crystal and will be washed with cold water, then dried in the shade. The stones which were set aside earlier are then mixed with the same. Then you take three pounds of tartar dregs of white wine, and cook it in a crucible with thirty pints of forge water- add to it eight ounces of salt niter and an ounce of ivy juice, and place the crystal therein. It must be boiled all together as you have done heretofore; And when the composition will be reduced by one third, skim the crust off the surface and continue to boil until, by the same test as mentioned before, everything is mixed fully. A barrel must be obtained, one with numerous sticks inside lengthwise, with a place at the bottom four fingers high which shall be empty, to make a space for the matter which will precipitate upwards onto the sticks. Close the barrel with the material inside and encase it in hot manure for fifteen days to give the borax time to crystallize on the sticks. This will multiply the material fourfold and serve just as well as imported, pure borax.

Creating Imitation Pearls

You will take four ounces of the finest and most white seed beads you can find: the bigger the better. Now place them in pure water with alum and mix it for the space of a quarter of an hour with an ivory spatula. When the material is of a thick consistency, you will wash it gently with distilled rain water and having evaporated the water on hot coals, you again mix the beans with the water. Then you must put the thick material in a small glass vessel, well sealed, and when this has digested in hot manure for two weeks, you will form beads with this paste in a silver mold: it will be good to observe that the mold contains four or five openings to form many pearls, and they are not all of the same figure, that is to say, they are a little more or less round than one the other, to better mimic the natural; we pierce them while they are soft, with silk or hair.

Hang them in a well stopped container to dry, lest the air alters them, and you will heat this gently to speed the process. After six hours, you will remove the pearls, and have them all separately wrapped in silver leaf. Now heat the pearls in a mash of dough without butter or shortening.

When you withdraw the pearls, if they appear not to have enough luster, you will them wash five or six times in a row with distilled water with the following; graculi grass, bean flowers, powdered rock alum, galena, plantain leaves well macerated, and a small amount of saltpeter. Finally, to harden them so that they appear natural, you will make a paste as follows. Take one ounce and a half of good scale, an ounce of Roman vitriol, six egg whites, and boil this for a half hour in plantain water, and you will mix it all together in a still with distilled water. Form a paste with barley flour last of all, in a silk screen, and wrap your pearls in a small white linen, and bake them in this paste, and be convinced that if you observe all these things accurately, you will have made pearls of great value able to deceive even the most skilled.

To Create Fake Musk That Will Be Seen As Real Musk

You will have an aviary or small loft well exposed to the rising sun, in a gay place, and you will put six hairy pigeons therein, preferably black ones, and all males, and you will begin on the last three days of the moon to give seed aspic instead of other seeds that they are usually fed, and instead of common water, you will give them drinks of rose water. Then the first day of the next moon, you feed them in the following manner; you have a paste made of powdered beans, about the weight of six pounds, mixed with rose water and the specified powders below; namely, flowers of spica nardi and calami aromatici, each six drachmas in weight, with good cinnamon, good cloves, nutmeg and ginger, each six drachmas in weight, all reduced to a fine powder. You will form this paste into grains, the size of a chickpea, and shall dry them in the sun, lest they become moldy; you give these to the pigeons four times a day, feeding each one six of these pellets every time, continuing this work for the space of eighteen days, and they should drink rose water, and you must take care of them properly, cleaning their droppings properly and such. After that time you will have an earthen vessel, glazed, and cut the neck of each of your pigeons, putting their blood in the vessel, which you should have weighed beforehand, so you can find out just how much blood there will be in that vessel. After you have removed the bits of feather which will be on the blood, add a bit of oriental musk mixed with rose water- there must be at least one drachma of musk and rosewater to every three ounces of blood, with six drops of gall beef added to all the rest, and then must place the vessel in a larger, luted one, and warm this mix for fifteen days in hot horse manure. It will however be better to do this digestion in summer under the hot sun as well, and when you see that the matter will be well dried in the vessel, store it in cotton in a fine lead box. This creates artificial musk so good that it will pass for the finest oriental musk. And by this means one can make considerable savings by frequently doing this, since the increase of matter here will exceed perhaps thirty ounces.

Making Fake Ambergris

You will reduce to a fine powder the following substances and pass them through a fine sieve; namely, an ounce of starch, an ounce of iris, half an ounce of asphaltum, an ounce of benzoin, one ounce and a half of whale semen, and a good dram of musk from the East, which shall be dissolved in cinnamon water, and you'll soak a bit of tragacanth in this cinnamon water, and all this will form a paste that you put in digestion under horse manure, as it was said of musk and, when you observe that it is sufficiently dry, you will keep it for use in a box with cotton, to keep it fresh. It can be exposed to air and will store in this way for up to ten years.

Making Excellent Incense Pellets

You will take four ounces of benzoin, two ounces of

storax, and a quarter ounce of aloe wood. Boil this all on low heat for half an hour in a glazed vessel, with the rose water, such that the rose water exceeds rise above the rest of the material by a depth of two fingers. Now cool the mix and drain off the remaining fluid to use for soaking the next ingredients. Take dried pomace, and grind it to a fine powder with lime mortar and a good pound of willow charcoal; then soak gum tragacanth in the water you have kept from before; then join your powders with a good dram of oriental musk, dissolved in a little rose water. Make a paste of it, which you will form into pellets the length and thickness of your little finger, forming them in a tapered manner with a flatter bottom so they can be stood up straight. When well dried, the pointy end is lit, making good incense. To make them even better, add six grains of good ambergris.

Softening Ivory

It is sometimes amazing to foreigners how excellent ivory works are sold here for such a low price. It might not be so if we had not found the secret to soften ivory, and to mold it, and by so doing in one hour what one might elsewhere do in a week. Here is what I learned from a skilled artist from the city of Dantzic. One must take a piece of ivory of pure white; then it is boiled in sea water clarified by filtration with six ounces of mandrake root, and it shall be tested with a rod to see if it is sufficiently soft to be pressed into a mold, while still warm and very clean. When the mold is full, it is allowed to cool and then the figure is allowed to harden for two or three days.

THE PETIT ALBERT

Obtaining Grass Twine

Find the perch of a crow or any other bird which is annoying to you. Coil some rope in that spot such that the mother can come there to feed her chicks; then spread some sheets below the nest. The bird will pick at the ropes and bits of fabric will fall from the nest as it does, as the bird rejects the ropes which to it are a nuisance. You can take these bits of fabric to do with whatever you wish.

Breaking Iron Easily

You will take reduced soap sticks, a little thick in width, and anoint the iron bar; then you will clean the place where you want the bar to be broken, and with a brush you anoint five or six times this place with hot water. It will eat so suddenly through the iron, that in less than six hours of time you can easily break the bar in half.

A Ring That Heals Palsy

You will craft a pure silver ring, in which there is embedded a cat eye stone. Obtain a piece of horn for engraving the ring; then choose a Monday in spring when the moon will be favorable towards or in conjunction with Jupiter or Venus, and in the favorable time for the constellation; now you engrave inside the ring the following: "+ + Dhabi, Habi + + Haber, Habi +"; Then perfume it three times with the perfume of Monday. Rest assured that when worn on the middle finger it prevents and treats the falling sickness.

THE PETIT ALBERT

Talismans To Protect Against Dangerous Animals

The talisman that I will discuss is engraved heretofore, and is the first after seven mysterious number of planets; it is of a marvelous efficacy against poisons, giving the wearer a feeling when danger approaches, a feeling of pulsation, which warns of the danger. It is also very effective in preventing the bites of all venomous animals and insects. Here is the manner of its creation: Form a small plate of pure gold, purified and polished, on a Sunday, in the favorable time of the constellation; now engrave the figures that are represented in the model that I have given above; then use the perfume of Sunday to scent the plate three times, under the auspices of the Sun. Having wrapped the talisman in a cloth of suitable tissue, it should be kept in a small clean box: one can also burn on the back of the plate a Sun with its rays burning insects or toads, or other vermin.

Explanation and Engravings of the Talismans

I have placed the figures very accurately for these four talismans from the great original manuscript of the Imperial Library of Insbruck. The first representing a human face, with Hebrew characters, is good to conciliate the friendship of sprites, distributors of wealth and honors. It should be formed on a Sunday under the auspices of the Sun, on an end plate of gold, with the ceremonies of suitable perfume when the planets are in a favorable situation, and above all in good aspect with Jupiter.

The second, in which we see the figure of an arm

sticking out of a cloud, is to be formed on a Monday, under the auspices of the Moon, on a pure silver plate well polished, with proper ceremonies and perfume, and at the time of the favorable constellation. It is good to ensure travelers from all perils of land and sea, and mainly prevents attack by brigands, pirates, or pitfalls.

The third must be formed on Tuesday day under the auspices of the planet Mars, with ceremonies and the proper fragrance, and at the hour of good constellation, Mars in conjunction with Jupiter, or watched benignly over by Venus. It is very effective for successful military expeditions, to charm firearms, such that they will not backfire and harm the wearer; it must be engraved on an iron plate, purified and well polished.

The fourth is to be formed on the day of Wednesday, under the auspices of Mercury, made with Mercury on a thin plate fixed with proper ceremonies and perfume, with the planet at the time of good constellation, Mercury being in conjunction or in benign appearance with Venus or the Moon. The virtue and property of this talisman is to make one wealthy in games and stocks; it also ensures travelers against thieves, and dissipates or discovers betrayal formed against the life of the person who is provided with its use.

Argent Vive Of Hungary

You put into a still a pound and a half of good fresh rosemary flowers, a half pound of pouillot flowers, a half pound of marjoram flowers, a half pound of lavender flowers, and above all three pints of good living water; with the still sealed well to prevent evaporation, you will put it for twenty four hours digestion in a pile of hot horse manure; then you will put the same in a distilled water bath. The use of this water is to take it one or two times a week, with a morning fasting, about the amount of one drachma, and to wash the face with it mixed with any other liquer, and to wash any part of the body with any physical complaint as well. This remedy renews the strength, makes the mind clear, dispelling distractions, confirms the health until the decrepitude of old age, makes a person look younger, is admirable for the stomach and chest , rubbing in the above: this remedy should be kept cool. This recipe is was given to Isabella, Queen of Hungary, for her own use.

Making A Wash To Cure Facial Blemishes

Take saltpeter and wrap it in a thin cloth; soaking the same with pure water. Touch your blemishes with this cloth soaked as said. There is also a water that is a good use to beautify the face, and I advise this method more readily than what I just said regarding saltpeter. You will take two quarts of water in which you cooked Fajolles beans, until they are reduced almost to a paste; this water is then put into a still. You shall join two bundles of chickweed, two of silverweed, one pound of ground veal, with six fresh eggs, and to all this a pint of white vinegar. You distill this mixing in a water bath, and you'll have made an excellent water to dispel blemishes, washing with the same in the evening and the morning. I know there are countless people who fear that these distillations will not restore youth; but here is one that has such an effect, smoothing the skin: You

THE PETIT ALBERT

mix bread with three pounds of wheat flour, beans flour, a pound of goat's milk, with mild sourdough; when you have baked the same mix, you shall dissolve any crumbs by adding new milk cheese and six egg whites with a sponge. Add one ounce of calcined shell egg and mix this all together in a still. You will make a distillation of this with fire, and you will have an excellent rejuvenating water, rubbing your face every day with the same, it will make the skin polished like a mirror. It will also whiten the skin as well, using the true water of Venice, which is done in the following manner. You will take two pints of milk, the blood of a black cow taken in May, a pint of water from a grape vine bleeding its sap, four lemons with four oranges, slicing the same, with two ounces of candy sugar, half an ounce of well pulverized borax, four onions pounded thoroughly, and narcissus bulb, and you put all this together to distill and cook in a water bath, and you will keep this water in a bottle well corked.

A Powder To Exfoliate The Face

You will take thirty sheep hooves and six hooves from calves. You must strip away all the flesh, which may take some time. You grind the bony hooves the best you can, and you will take good care to remove the marrow that you will find, cooking them all in a pot, skimming the foam gently to remove the debris and fats. When they are boiled for the space of three hours, you should cool them and chill the same; then with a silver spoon, fat will rise to the surface. Skim off and take this fat, and for every half pound of skimmed fats you'll add a dram of calcined borax and as much rock alum, with two ounces of grapeseed oil, and you'll boil it all together in a pint of white wine, which is very clear, and let it cool down. Take this fatty solid and wash it several times in rosewater until it becomes very white and powdery, and lay it in small pots for you to use as desired.

A Soap For Faces and Hands Alike

Take a pound of iris from Florence, four ounces of storax, two ounces of sallow sandalwood, half an ounce of cloves, half an ounce of fine cinnamon, and the same of nutmeg, with a grain of ambergris. All this is to be reduced to a powder and sieved with the ambergris powdered separately. Then take two pounds of good white soap, grate it into three pints of water spirits to soak for four or five days; then knead this with water in which oranges were boiled and you will make a paste with starch finely sieved into it. Now you can mix your ambergris dissolved with a little tragacanth liquefied in water. This paste you will form into bars of soap you then lay in the shade, and all of this should be stored in boxes with cotton for preservation.

Making Holy Water

Have a great alembic, in which you put the following materials: four ounces of benzoin, two ounces of storax, one ounce of sallow sandalwood, two ounces of cloves, two or three pieces of iris from Florence, half of lemon peel, two nutmeg nuts, a half ounce of cinnamon, two quarts of good mineral water, a pint of orange flower water, a pint of sweet clover water. You put everything in a still properly sealed and distilled in a water bath. This distillation creates an exceedingly holy water.

The Light of the Hand of Glory

Take four ounces of the herb called Rauwolfia, put it in a sealed clay pot, then digest it; that is to say, in hot horse manure for two weeks, it will turn into small red strings, which you will add to an oil according to the principles of the art, and this oil you can place atop a lamp. When it above a lamp in a room, it will cause all those there to sleep deeply such that they will hardly be able to awake.

A Secret Compass For Long Distance Communication

Make two stainless steel boxes that are of the same weight, height and face, with a large enough edge to put all around it various symbols as needed; there should be a pivot at the bottom as found on any ordinary compass. Take care that your boxes are well polished and spotless; then look for several stones of good magnetic quality, that is, having a side which tends to point south, having white veins. Find whichever such stone is long and shows a powerful magnetic ability, and carve it down to make it two needles in your two boxes, making them as similar and fine as you are able; they must be of the same thickness and of a same weight, with a small hole therein, to put them on the pivot in balance. This so prepared, you give one of these boxes to your friend, with whom you want to link correspondence, and will mark him within an hour in any day of the week, even one hour of every day if desired; and more if we wants, but this is a little annoying because whenever you wish to communicate you must be in his area for fifteen minutes or half an hour, or an hour even before the one you assigned to your friend. When this is first done there needs to be a cross, or some mark for the beginning of the alphabet, to calibrate both boxes properly at that time. As these two needles are from one stone, operating the device is as simple as one of you turning the needle to a letter or symbol on their box, and the other person's box will then mark the same, allowing one way communication. When the other answers, it is done similarly. The box and needle should be kept separated by cotton in a good box, and rust must be avoided at all costs to prevent the device from being useless.

To Fire a Rifle With Great Accuracy and Power

Take two ounces of good gunpowder, put an ounce of coarsely crushed white pepper in it, and mix everything well; load your rifle with a little more than the regular powder load, and over the powder put a bit of camphor before your fight. Turn over the ball wrapped with paper and brush the barrel. You may also use an herb called psyllium; it is a seed that is gathered under Leo: it has a little seed like mustard. It is burnt in the barrel of the gun, while it is forged, and then it is ready for use.

A Serum To Preserve Life

Take eight pounds of mercurial juice, the juice of two pounds of borage, twelve pounds of honey from Narbonne or another, the best in the country, and boil this all together; heat and filter it for clarity. Set it aside.

THE PETIT ALBERT

Set aside to infuse for twenty four hours the following; four ounces of gentian root, cut by slices in three pints of white wine on hot ashes, stirring from time to time; you will pass the wine through a filter but not a press.

Put this second mix in those juices with honey, making it all boil gently yet again, and cook it until it has a syrup consistency; Place them all in a bowl to cool, then bottle the same, taking a spoonful every morning for your health.

The syrup which I speak of here protects the memory, prolongs life, restores health against all kinds of diseases, even gout, dissipates heat from the bowels- it also heals pulmonary complaints, it is good for stomach pain, for sciatica, dizziness, migraine, and usually for internal pain.

Taking only every morning a spoonful of the syrup, you can be sure not to need a doctor or apothecary. It brings lifelong health because it has such a virtue, it can not suffer corruption or bad mood in the body, evacuating it therefrom.

This secret was given by a poor peasant, Calabria, one who was appointed by Charles V, to his general in the navy which was sent to Barbary; the good man was 132 years old, as he said to this general, who had gone to stay with him. Seeing such a great age, the general inquired his way of living and that of several of his neighbors, who were all aged almost like him; they looked to be at most thirty years old, and were even given to a libertine

THE PETIT ALBERT

disposition.

A count of Germany, ill for thirteen years, was healed; Voter Bavarian condemned and abandoned by the Empire's doctors, the Marchioness of Brandenburg, paralyzed for nine years, the Duchess of Freiburg remained in languor after a long illness, and several other quality people whose numbers almost infinite; Finally, those who have used it, are made happier by its power.

Planting Tree Branches To Make Them Grow

You should cut a branch of whatever tree you wish- but a deciduous tree, not a pine or spruce- a cutting of two or three fingers' breadth. Put an oat seed under the planting, and one at each bud, and then place the graft into the soil.

Making Much Soap

Take ten pots of water, six pounds of Alicante liquer, and two pounds of almond hulls reduced to ash; all this together makes a detergent that you will keep aside.

Take ten pounds of soap cut into pieces, put them in a boiler over a low heat until melted. When this is done, pour over the same ten pounds of your former mix, and boil this together for ten eleven times. Now take starch and pour it into the cauldron where the soap is melted, and stir everything well. Boil it all and then afterward have a wooden box and put some lime in the same, then pour in the melted material, and let it dry in the shade and air it out.

Note that the starch is only whitening material to make the soap white.

Increasing Saffron

Take one ounce and a half of water spirits, two drachmas of fine sugar, and a half drachma of saltpeter; put it all on fire, and add it in one ounce of saffron. After stirring said decoction, let it dry in the sun, and you will enjoy a nice increase.

Increasing Black Pepper

Mingle the pepper with cardamom seed, or else with grains of paradise.

Increasing Wax

Take ten pounds of white wax, and cook it. Being melted, three pounds of well sifted flour of iris are added. Stir it with a wooden spoon thoroughly and let it cool.

Increasing Musk

Take rhubarb stems, preferably the oldest and most rotten of them, and macerate or grind it into powder or small pieces. Boil and stir the same until it has the consistency of a treacle. Let it dry by itself in the shade. Mix it with your musk.

THE PETIT ALBERT

Dying Hair

Take litharge powder, put it in water and stir well with a stick, heating it, and in the hot water put your hair: if you put too little litharge, the color will not be so strong; if you put a lot, it will be stronger; it is not necessary to boil the water, simply make sure that everything is heated through. After it, it will instead be done, but not so well.

Making A Fine Gold Varnish

Use two pints of wine spirits well filtered or if you want, a little more. If you want the varnish to be a bit less red, you can also reduce the weight with a little shellac, which is red.

Take four ounces of shellac grain, two ounces of gamboge powder in a vial, with your wine spirits, and reduce the same to one third volume over a fire pit. To use it, apply the varnish to your wood, metal, paper, or whatever, then put a layer of metal over it leaving everything to dry. When it is dry, you still put a layer of said coating on the sheet of said metal, and let it dry again, continuing until your gilding takes on the color you desire. You will not need a brush for this varnishing method.

Healing A Husky Throat

Take a quart of rain water, two tablespoons of pot barley, and a piece of licorice, long as the hand, beaten flat. Soak it all day, then boil it until the barley begins to dissolve. Take this every morning and evening, four spoonfuls with eight spoonfuls of fresh milk.

Cleaning the Teeth and Gums

Take an ounce of well crushed myrrh, two spoonfuls of white honey of the best quality, and some good sage, and you rub your teeth morning and evening with this.

Preventing Foul Breath

Take a bit of myrrh before going to bed and hold it in your mouth, such that it dissolves.

Curing A Bad Fever

Take blessed thistle, absinthe wormwood, and saffron. Steep it in boiling water and drink it in the same way as tea, every day, or a bit more as a fever begins, and you will be healed.

A Secret To Maintain Good Health

At noon each day, take four rue stems, nine grains of juniper, a nut, a dry fig, and a little salt; mash it all together and eat it on an empty stomach.

To Determine Whether A Patient Shall Live or Die

There are many ways used to determine whether a patient will live or die; but I will publish this infallible sign which can serve one and all, and make a firm judgment of the same. Take a nettle and steep it in the urine of the

THE PETIT ALBERT

patient, forthwith after the patient will have urinated, and let the nettle sit there for twenty four hours. If the nettle is dry at that time the patient will die. If it is not dry, the patient will live.

Curing Dropsy

This disease is caused by Saturn; thus observe that it is the hour of Mars or Venus, and take the grass named martarique. Grind it up and mix it with the yolk of a boiled egg into an omelette, and eat it on an empty stomach, this will preserve you from dropsy and gout.

Curing Fistulas

This disease is caused by Mars; thus observe that it is the hour of Saturn or Jupiter and take powdered lilyturf root, mixed with the ashes of burnt oysters, and some pig fat, and you will apply this mix to the fistula.

Curing Pox Scars

This disease is caused by Mars; thus observe that it is the hour of the Moon, Mercury, Saturn or Jupiter. Take litharge, dried cane root, chickpea flour, and grain flour; crush and mix this all with almond oil and melted sheep fat. Anoint the face with it in the morning and evening and wash with hot water.

Curing Bladder Stones

This disease is caused by the Moon; thus observe

THE PETIT ALBERT

that it is the hour of Mars or Mercury. Take scorpions, put them in a new earthen pot that has a narrow mouth, and put it in an oven that is not too hot. In six hours, crush the baked scorpions and eat them

Curing Colic

This disease is caused by the Moon; thus observe that it is the hour of Mars or Mercury. Take the laurel fruit, and make it into a powder, and add two drachmas of weight of the same to aromatic wine; it will take away the pain.

Curing Urination Problems

This disease is caused by the Moon; thus observe that it is the hour of Mars or Mercury. Take the seeds of abrotanus, and boil them in water. Add a decoction of cantharide beetles without head, feet and wings. Let the powder settle and drink a spoonful to urinate.

Curing Oedemas

This disease is caused Saturn; thus observe that it is the hour of Mars or Venus. Take a pheasant, kill it and drain the blood;. Drink two glasses of the same and the disease will be healed.

Curing Stomach Pains

This disease is caused by the Sun; thus observe that it is the hour of Mars, Mercury or the Moon. Take a chicken and kill it, and remove the stones from its belly and powder them. Drink this with wine for a cure.

THE END

Printed in Great Britain
by Amazon